DOWN CAME

CAME

THE RAIN

DOWN

CAME

THE RAIN

A mother's story of
depression and recovery

BROOKE SHIELDS

MICHAEL JOSEPH
an imprint of
PENGUIN BOOKS

MICHAEL JOSEPH

Published by the Penguin Group
Penguin Books Ltd, 80 Strand, London WC2R 0RL, England
Penguin Group (USA) Inc., 375 Hudson Street, New York, New York 10014, USA
Penguin Group (Canada), 10 Alcorn Avenue, Toronto, Ontario, Canada M4V 3B2
(a division of Pearson Penguin Canada Inc.)
Penguin Ireland, 25 St Stephen's Green, Dublin 2, Ireland (a division of Penguin Books Ltd)
Penguin Group (Australia), 250 Camberwell Road,
Camberwell, Victoria 3124, Australia (a division of Pearson Australia Group Pty Ltd)
Penguin Books India Pvt Ltd, 11 Community Centre,
Panchsheel Park, New Delhi – 110 017, India
Penguin Group (NZ), cnr Airborne and Rosedale Roads, Albany,
Auckland 1310, New Zealand (a division of Pearson New Zealand Ltd)
Penguin Books (South Africa) (Pty) Ltd, 24 Sturdee Avenue,
Rosebank 2196, South Africa

Penguin Books Ltd, Registered Offices: 80 Strand, London WC2R 0RL, England

www.penguin.com

First published in the United States of America by Hyperion Books 2005
First published in Great Britain by Michael Joseph 2005

1

Printed in Great Britain by Clays Ltd, St Ives plc

A CIP catalogue record for this book is available from the British Library

ISBN 0–718–14841–X

To my daughter,

Rowan,

who makes life worth living

CONTENTS

ACKNOWLEDGMENTS

I want to express my love and appreciation to my amazing husband, Chris, for continuing to show me what true love is. My deepest thanks to my dear friend and constant support John Kimble, who said, "You just have to write this book," and to Kassie Evashevski, who steered me in the right direction and made it happen. To my editors, Mary Ellen O'Neill and Mindy Werner: Thank you for always keeping me on track and helping me to complete the daunting task of writing this book.

Finally, thanks to Dr. Joyce Vargyas, Dr. Andrei Rebarber, and Dr. Shari Lusskin for their support and expertise with regard to my journey into motherhood.

DOWN
CAME
THE RAIN

Once upon a time, there was a little girl who dreamed of being a mommy. She wanted, more than anything, to have a child and knew her dream would come true one day. She would sit for hours thinking up names to call her baby.

Eventually this little girl grew up. Though she'd met and married her Prince Charming, she was having trouble conceiving. She began to realize that her dream wasn't going to come true without a great deal of medical help.

So she went on a long journey through the world of fertility treatments. When none of them worked, she got frustrated and depressed. She felt like a failure.

And then one day, finally, she became pregnant. She was thrilled beyond belief. She had a wonderful pregnancy and a perfect baby girl. At long last, her dream of being a mommy had come true. But instead of being relieved and happy, all she could do was cry.

CHAPTER 1

THE LITTLE ENGINE THAT COULD

AFTER ALL OF THE TIME I've spent in the public eye, you might think that finding out I was going to have a miscarriage moments before stepping onstage wouldn't shake me up, but it did....

December 2001. I'm standing in the wings of the Palace Theatre in Hollywood, California, for MuppetFest, which is a tribute to Jim Henson as well as a fund-raiser for Save the Children. I'm wearing a sleeveless black sequined dress and am in full hair and makeup. There is a great deal of excitement and energy in the air, and the audience, a full house, is having difficulty staying quiet. From where I'm standing, I can see lots of grown-ups and kids milling around their seats, eating popcorn and talking.

In order not to be seen by the audience before my cue, I have to move farther backstage, to where Mr. Snuffleupagus is also waiting for his entrance. However, because he is such an oversize creature, he is too big to make room for me. I end up having to wedge myself under his chin and between his front legs. Little bits of brown fur are flying everywhere, including up my nose. It takes all my effort not to sneeze.

It won't be long before the stage will be filled with color and sound and lots and lots of fur. So here I am, wearing a pink feather boa and long purple gloves and a huge fake diamond ring that keeps getting caught on the boa. And though it's not yet evident, I'm pregnant. But it's not that simple. Yesterday, after some basic blood work, I was told that for some reason, something wasn't right with the pregnancy, and additional testing was needed. I was reassured that it was a routine precaution. So, early this morning, before coming to the theater, I went back to the clinic to have more blood drawn. And while I was rehearsing, trying not to think about it, the technicians were analyzing my blood.

Now, while I'm waiting for my cue, my cell phone rings. The news is not good. My doctor says, "I'm sorry, but the pregnancy is no longer viable." I start to get very warm, and a huge lump forms in my throat. My doctor delicately explains that it is "nature's way" of saying the baby isn't strong enough to survive, and it's better to have it happen sooner rather than later. There is a pause, and then she carefully adds that I am going to have to wait for my body to naturally expel the pregnancy or reabsorb it.

"What!" I can hardly grasp what I am hearing, and my vision begins to narrow. Just then another call comes through. It's my husband, Chris, wanting to know if I have heard any news. Almost mechanically, I relay the information. I want to throw the phone across the stage and run out sobbing, but I am surrounded by hairy creatures and can't leave.

At this moment I need to go onstage, decked out in a crazy costume, complete with a pig nose, à la Miss Piggy. Did I mention I am pretending to be Miss Piggy and I'm singing a duet with Kermit the Frog? As I move away from Snuffy's legs and look up at him, he is sympathetically blinking his huge eyelashes at me. The stage manager can tell that something is wrong as I wipe tears from my face, but he has no choice other than to cue the Muppet rock band to file onto the stage and then point at me for my entrance. As they say, the show must go on.

I HAD ALWAYS wanted to have children, and like most people, I just assumed it would happen when the time was right. My parents were divorced when I was quite young, and my mom never remarried. I was an only child in my mother's house, and I used to beg her to adopt a baby. I desperately wanted a brother or sister to play with and take care of. My mother never did adopt a child, but my father remarried. Because my stepmother already had two children from a previous marriage, I had instant siblings. Then, luckily for me, my dad and stepmother added three wonderful daughters to the family. As a result, I was able to maintain a privileged, only-child status with my mom while enjoying being part of a larger family with my dad.

Years have a way of flying by, and before I knew it, my four years of college were over. Since I had been working basically since I was eleven months old, I significantly cut back on the number of jobs I took while I was at school. It was a much needed break. I graduated with a degree in French literature and then went back to working full-time. After a few years of living on my own in Manhattan, I met, dated, and subsequently married my first husband, Andre Agassi. We were busy with our individual careers, and our schedules often conflicted. Though we both wanted to have children, the appropriate time never seemed to present itself. Even though a great deal of love existed between the two of us, over time our lives seemed to become polarized and after two years, our marriage ended. It was a sad but amicable parting, and it was a blessing there were no children involved.

The real blessing, however, was that I was able to meet and fall in love with Chris Henchy, a comedy writer. To this day I believe that I fell in love with Chris the day we met, in 1999, but I would never tell him that! I had just gotten an American bulldog, Darla, and I brought her to meet friends of mine in the gym on the Warner Bros. lot. While there, the dog wandered off, and Chris brought her back. He was writing for a show filmed on the lot and loved dogs. We chatted and he made me laugh. I left without even knowing his full name, but he made such a strong impression that I called up a friend and told her I had found a guy I thought she should go out with. She told me she had starting seeing someone else. Because I had recently gotten divorced, I wasn't even considering dating. Three weeks later, I was hosting a show in Washington, D.C., for which Chris was the writer, and we started spending time together and became friends. I was struck by how thoughtful and funny he was. Because he knew my situation, there was no pressure, and we were just friends for quite some time. Finally, though, I had to admit that there was something between us that I could no longer ignore, and we started dating. Although we were each consumed by our individual jobs, he with writing and I with the last season of *Suddenly Susan*, we were both also quite ready to start a family.

Chris and I dated for two years and then became engaged. I was so clear about wanting to have children with this man that I would've gladly adjusted our plans if it happened before we were married. Though we didn't specifically try to have a baby, I chose to go off the pill. As the wedding approached, however, I wasn't getting pregnant. It crossed our minds that there might be something wrong. Wanting everything to be in order before we got married, we decided to see a fertility specialist in Los Angeles named Dr. Joyce Vargyas. She performed several tests and an examination, determining that changes in my cervix were probably the reason why I wasn't getting pregnant. Several years before, I'd had cervical surgery to remove precancerous cells, resulting in scarring that caused my cervix to be tight and significantly shortened.

As a result, the entrance to my uterus had become severely impeded, making it very difficult for me to get pregnant. In the process of removing the precancerous cells, the surgery also removed the cervical glands that secrete the mucus necessary to transport the sperm. Without this bodily fluid, the "little spermies," as one of the nurses affectionately called them, couldn't swim upstream. I said, "No wonder it hasn't been working—not only is the door closed, but the poor guys have been jumping into a pool with no water!" Dr. Vargyas reassured us that this was one of the easiest fertility issues to overcome, though she did mention the possibility of my cervix becoming incompetent during pregnancy and prematurely opening up. After hearing the word "incompetent," I couldn't help feeling like damaged goods. With a very serious expression, Chris said to my physician, "Please, Doctor, we don't like to use the word 'incompetent' in our house. Could you just say she has a 'special' cervix, or that she is simply 'cervically challenged'?"

Anxious to get started, we decided to try artificial insemination. In this procedure, which is done at the time of ovulation, the doctor inserts a catheter into the vagina, bypassing the scarred and narrowed tissue and putting the sperm directly into the uterus. Medically, it wasn't any different from having sex—at least from the sperm and egg's point of view (Chris begged to differ). After a couple of attempts, I still wasn't "knocked up." The doctor kept saying that it was the scarring on my cervix that was creating the difficulty and repeatedly making insemination unsuccessful. My eggs themselves, according to more ultrasounds, were looking very young and healthy. I was a fertile female. But it was suggested that even the thinnest catheter could not place the "stuff" where it needed to be. I tried to find comfort in the fact that at least my eggs were in good shape.

Soon Chris and I were given some additional surprising news. My doctor indicated that because of my age, I didn't have the luxury of time. She tactfully said that my biological clock was ticking and that it not only took time to have children, but if we wanted more than one, we needed to think about a more aggressive approach. The next step should be an in vitro fertilization procedure.

"IVF?" I blurted out. "Isn't that for older women? I'm only thirty-six. You said I was fertile and healthy!"

I admit, it was strange being informed that I was almost too old for something when I was in good shape and felt like a spring chicken. Undergoing IVF would mean enduring an involved and arduous series of procedures. It entailed drugs, shots, and surgery. This was quite upsetting to us, but it looked like we didn't have a choice. Chris and I figured that if this was indeed the path we needed to take, then we would have to mentally and physically prepare for it. We spent a lot of time educating ourselves about the entire process.

At first I shared this news only with a friend who had gone through IVF herself and was currently pregnant. She was so positive about the whole thing that we were encouraged. Soon we told our parents that we were availing ourselves of modern medicine and that they would get a grandchild out of it. Meanwhile, Dr. Vargyas was convinced that we would have our baby in no time.

Around this time, I was offered the chance to play Sally Bowles, the lead character in *Cabaret*, on Broadway. Sally and I could not have been more opposite. In the play, she becomes pregnant by accident and is forced to make a crucial decision. I was trying to get pregnant, and if it were to happen, it would be anything but an accident. Still, the focus on babies and birth struck me as ironic. However, I couldn't survive eight shows a week for six months if I did get pregnant (I was not going to be that Method), so I, too, had a choice to make. Chris and I discussed what a wonderful and rewarding opportunity doing such a tough play would be, and we felt it would be good for me to take the job. We had not yet begun IVF, and the wedding was getting close. Once all the festivities had passed and my run in the play was over, I could then begin the fertility treatments. We thought this new schedule was going to work perfectly.

I accepted the part with excitement and a healthy fear. It would be the most challenging role I had ever taken, and I was invigorated by the prospect of playing it. I decided I would use my time wisely. I would get myself into the best possible shape for the character and fully commit to the experience of *Cabaret*. The physical preparedness and stamina necessary to sustain a Broadway schedule would be daunting, but it would surely be helpful in getting ready for the rigors of in vitro.

ON MAY 26, 2001, Chris and I were married in Palm Beach, Florida. My dad, who lived there and had been diagnosed with late-stage prostate cancer, was unable to travel because of his chemotherapy treatments. So we decided to forgo getting married in New York, as originally planned, and invited a smaller group of people to travel to Florida, where we got married at the home of my father's close friend, facing the ocean.

The wedding was everything we had hoped for. The weather held, despite the threat of rain, and there was enough of a breeze that it was never too warm. The ceremony was timed for sunset, and as it began, Tuck & Patti (a powerful musical team whom I have loved and followed for years) performed "Heaven Down Here." We had written our own vows, and the service was intimate and spiritual without being heavy. By the time we got to the reception, when our comedian friends were trying to top one another in the joke department during their toasts, everyone was smiling. After dinner we had our first dance as "Mr. and Mrs." And then I danced with my father. It was the last time I would ever dance with him, and I cherish the photo I have of us. The next day we continued the party with a barbecue on the lawn. Chris and I left the following day for a two-week trip to Fiji and Bali. A week after we returned from our honeymoon, I went straight into the two-week rehearsal period for *Cabaret*.

Two weeks is hardly enough time to learn a whole show, and I was practically paralyzed by the thought of opening on the Great White Way after only fourteen days of rehearsal. I had been on Broadway before, in the revival of *Grease*, but the cast was much bigger and I only had two solos. I had five solo numbers in *Cabaret* and, as the lead, was following in some impressive footsteps.

I stayed at my New York apartment, and Chris had to commute from Los Angeles to visit me on weekends. A bicoastal existence was not new to me, but it was a relatively novel one for my husband. Chris would be the one doing all of the traveling, but I justified it for him by saying, "Think of the frequent-flyer miles you'll rack up." We knew the schedule would be a bit hard on us as newlyweds, but starring on Broadway was such an incredible opportunity, and Chris strongly supported it. Miraculously, we survived. It turned out to be an unbelievably rewarding experience.

As it happened, I was doing *Cabaret* in September 2001. I was alone on the eleventh, because Chris hadn't planned to fly out until the weekend. I was awakened by a phone call from my friend Sherie, who said a plane had just hit the World Trade Center. I went into a state of shock. I turned on the TV. At that point, the reporters were still saying that it had been just a small commuter plane. I turned off the TV and headed outside. As I got to the street, I saw crowds of people all walking frantically: My apartment was next to the UN, which had been evacuated. It was so chaotic. I called Chris from my cell phone, and he told me to go home immediately, that the second tower had been hit. Although I'd been walking around in a daze, once I got home, I was too agitated to stay there, so I left and walked the few miles to a friend's apartment. But I couldn't stay, so I headed back home. After leaving and coming back home two more times, I ended up at my sister Marina's house. I'd spoken to my parents, but soon all the circuits were busy, and I could no longer use my cell phone. I kept trying to reach Chris, and very late at night I got through. All I could do was cry. He reassured me that he would get to me as soon as he could.

Mayor Rudolph Guiliani wanted Broadway to reopen on Thursday, September 13. *Cabaret* was one of the first shows back on, and it was a sad, sad show. We did the performance for an audience of sixty-eight people as opposed to the thousand who normally filled the seats. After the show was finished, it was quiet. There wasn't even any applause. The audience got to their feet and mouthed the words "Thank you." Later the next week, a number of us from the cast went down to Ground Zero after the show and cooked breakfast until five in the morning. We didn't know what else to do to help out. After walking through the devastating wreckage together, we started talking about the importance of family and of being surrounded by those you love. I missed my husband terribly and was very scared. All I wanted was to be with him and to start our own family. I would have to wait another week before we would be reunited.

TOWARD THE END of my run in *Cabaret*, the doctor said that if I wanted to, I could begin taking some of the shots needed in preparation for IVF. It wouldn't hurt my performance at all and would speed up the process a bit. I decided to go ahead with it and started taking a drug called Lupron, which shuts down the body's natural production of hormones. My system needed to be a clean slate before it could be manipulated as part of the IVF treatment. All I would have to do was put a tiny needle underneath the surface of the skin on my thigh each night for a few weeks, and my entire reproductive system could soon be told what to do. It was actually the same drug my father had been taking to slow down the growth and spread of his prostate cancer. He and I were able to discuss our treatments, and when Dad came to see my final performance in the play, I joked with him about meeting me in the bathroom to "shoot up."

Dad and I also shared our experiences regarding the drug's side effects. He would call me daily in my dressing room before a show: "These drugs . . . I have such headaches, and the depression . . . oh boy . . . but you know what it's like, you know what I'm talking about, right?" He never called just to complain, but I could tell he was scared and needed to talk. It was comforting for me to be able to respond with "Oh my God, Dad, you get it, and how about the hot flashes and fatigue?" In an odd way, I believe it was a relief to my father not to be completely alone in his treatment. My condition was not grave, like his, nor was I fighting to stay alive. And although it was sad, it was also somehow a much needed way for us to identify with each other. I must admit that I clung to this thought, especially when I couldn't be at his bedside during his last moments. It struck me as ironic that I had been taking the drug in an effort to create a new life while he was taking it at the end of his.

I was to take the Lupron for the few weeks prior to beginning the next series of shots, which would happen once the play was over and I had returned to Los Angeles. As promised, the medicine didn't affect my performance at all, and luckily, I could easily administer it myself. It was, however, a sight to behold. Just after the curtain call each night, my dresser (the person who preps the entire wardrobe and helps with all of the fast changes) would lay out a syringe and a beer on my dressing table and say, "Come on, druggie." There I would sit, topless, dressed only in stockings and silver shoes, with my hair in a wig cap, black eyeliner smudged all down my face, white body makeup and bruised red veins painted on my body, the strap of a mike pack Velcroed around my ribs, sticking a needle into my thigh. It was almost fitting, given the ambience of the play, but a shocking image nonetheless. I looked like a character from *Trainspotting* or *A Clockwork Orange*.

Those last few weeks flew by, and I had an extremely emotional final performance. As a cast, we had shared a great deal together, and strong friendships had been forged. It would be strange not going to the theater every day. After an intense six months, I was heartbroken to leave the show, but I was fortified by the notion that I was about to begin an even more incredible journey.

I returned to Los Angeles feeling unbelievably strong and physically ready to do what was necessary to become pregnant. Though I had anticipated that I'd be in top physical shape by the end of the play, I hadn't expected to undergo such an emotional transformation. I felt more confident and peaceful than I had in a long while. This, I decided, could only be a good thing when trying to get pregnant.

Since Chris and I would be together every day, he could help me with the next series of IVF shots. These would stimulate my ovaries to produce multiple eggs and ensure that ovulation would not occur until necessary. Chris had to give me these new shots, because when I tried, I literally froze. These drugs had to be injected into muscle, so the needles were much longer than the ones used to inject the Lupron, and they had to go in places that were harder to reach. Chris was leery in the beginning, since the sight of needles usually made him very nervous. Whenever he had to get a shot, his nervousness would cause him to laugh to the point of hysteria, and it would take forever to get him still.

The day of my first rear-end shot, he later confessed, he almost passed out. He saw how big the needle was and how far it went into my body, but instead of laughing, he got sweaty and the room began to spin. Soon, however, he became a pro. Every morning and night, I would either bend over or push my stomach out to receive a different shot of medicine. Chris always tried to lighten the mood. At times he would pinch the desired spot and linger a bit longer than necessary before injecting the medicine. He would squeeze the top of my butt repeatedly, saying he had to "tenderize" the area properly. (I said he could tenderize it as long as he didn't bite it.) I was at his mercy, but laughter did make it less painful. I had to take these shots for weeks. In addition, there were countless doctor visits for blood tests, sonograms, and peeing on sticks, not to mention the estrogen patches I had to wear that made me look and feel like I'd had a skin graft when they were removed.

The whole process was quite an ordeal, and we became slaves to the time of day and to little vials of liquid. We'd find ourselves out at dinner with friends, and then we'd have to sneak off to a coat room, where we'd huddle over syringes and a travel-size cooler filled with small bottles of drugs. The smell of the alcohol pads would waft through the air, and people walking by would whisper. We imagined the headlines: BROOKE ON DRUGS, SEEN SHOOTING UP IN FANCY RESTAURANT! My husband and I were, needless to say, under a great deal of pressure, and emotions began running wild. One day, in the midst of my hormone bombardment, we were in a supermarket, and I burst into tears in one of the aisles. I couldn't articulate why I was crying, but commented that it was even more pathetic to be doing so in the canned-food section. Chris, not missing a beat, said, "Oh, honey, you want to cry in dairy, let's go cry in dairy." I didn't go to dairy, but I was beginning to see how the drugs were taking a toll.

Soon the shots were over and my many eggs were ready for their harvest. It was now time for phase two: surgery! At the hospital, I went through the pre-op procedure, got situated on my gurney, and was wheeled away. During surgery, the doctors retrieved all the eggs and then, through laparoscopy, placed two of them plus Chris's sperm in each fallopian tube. If all went well, fertilization and embryo development would subsequently take place in the middle of the tubes, where it naturally occurs. Appropriately, this procedure is called GIFT, or gamete intrafallopian tube transfer; it's a variation of the standard in vitro procedure. The rest of the extracted eggs were mixed with Chris's sperm in a petri dish. The ones that became fertilized would be frozen for later use.

After surgery, I woke up shaking from the anesthesia but recovered quickly. There was a chart clipped to my bed that said the transfer had been completed successfully and that my "tubes" were "pristine." It all sounded like pretty good news to me, even in my groggy state. I was sent to a hospital room to wake up a bit more before being discharged. I had to go to the bathroom and was positive I could make it on my own. Someone did have to come with me in case I fell, but I made sure I got off the gurney by myself. In front of the male attendant, a male nurse, and a couple of orderlies, I slid off and walked toward the bathroom with my head held high. What I wasn't aware of was that my hospital robe had twisted and was wide open in the back. My ass was wiggling in the open air, and it evidently also had sheet marks all over it from lying on the gurney. I had no idea about any of this and didn't even remember anybody coming into the bathroom with me to make sure I didn't end up in the toilet bowl. Chris was said to comment, "That's my wife."

We then went home to wait for the results. It would be two weeks before we could find out if an egg had fertilized and an embryo had implanted. I needed to stay calm. I tried to take it easy and refrained from exercise. I felt very positive and wanted to do everything right. I still had to keep the horrible estrogen patches on and was beginning to get itchy and inflamed welts where they were applied. None of it seemed to matter, because it was possible that I was pregnant.

Two weeks later, it was time for the blood test. Chris and I went to the clinic, and once again I gave the technician the most successful vein I had (one learns these things when blood tests are a daily occurrence). Chris had to return to work, and I had to find a way to stay busy until the results came back. I felt like a kid on Christmas morning. In a few hours, I got the call. In a cheery voice, the nurse said, "You're going to be a mommy." I couldn't believe my ears. It had all worked perfectly. I was ecstatic that I was actually pregnant. I began walking differently and touching my stomach constantly. I was immediately convinced that I had cravings. There were people to call and names to pick and classes to sign up for. When Chris arrived home, I had covered the floor with tiny plastic babies all leading to a big Keith Haring blow-up crawling baby. He followed the baby trail, and we cried and hugged and began calling our families. Our mothers immediately started saying that they didn't want to be called "Grandma." My mother-in-law wanted to be called "Cha Cha," and my mother came up with "Tootsie." (Don't ask!)

For the next few weeks, I had to go to the clinic each day for blood tests. I didn't mind all of the needle sticks, because I loved getting the results and watching my numbers steadily rise—until the day of my live performance with Kermit the Frog, when I got that awful call from the clinic.

AFTER MUPPETFEST, I came home from the theater and ripped the estrogen patch off so hard that I bled. I went to bed without discussing any of my feelings with my husband, not because he didn't want to talk but because I simply couldn't. The next day my doctor explained that a D&C was the usual procedure in a case like this, but it wasn't an option for me. Once again, because of my cervix, they wouldn't be able to get in there and get rid of the "no longer viable pregnancy." Opening my kind of cervix surgically might result in the even bigger problem of an incompetent cervix that couldn't be corrected. If that happened, I would never be able to carry a baby longer than four months. So I would have to wait for the pregnancy to completely die and for my body to expel it or reabsorb it.

By this time the self-pity was at an all-time high. Chris was very disappointed but said that miscarriages were more common than we realized and that it could have even happened to us before and we just weren't aware of it. It was harder for us now, because we had been looking at sonograms and hearing about the results of numerous blood tests every day. The anticipation had been building. He said the thing to do was to keep moving forward. I wanted to scream at him that he had no idea how it really felt, because he didn't have a uterus that had had a baby growing in it! I refrained from being so mean because I knew it was a loss to him as well. I cried and made angry calls to my mom, saying, "I'm not pregnant anymore. I lost it! I may just forget the whole thing." My mom usually gets the brunt of my bad moods, and she was going to get a healthy dose of venting from me for a while. I would've somehow tried to make the miscarriage her fault if I could have found a legitimate way to blame her. Thankfully, even at my worst, I didn't stoop that low.

I expressed my despair to many people close to me and then seriously confided to my girlfriend Stephanie that I really did fear it was some kind of cruel joke. Because I had been given so much in my life, had I reached my limit? Maybe I didn't deserve a child. She said I was letting my Catholic guilt get the better of me. Not only had I *not* had it that easy, but I did deserve to have a child. This calmed me down, and I tried to believe she was right.

Chris was sad, but more for my feelings than for the loss. He remained calm and said I wasn't being punished for anything. That baby was not supposed to happen for reasons we will probably never know, but instead of wasting any more time feeling sorry for myself, I should just jump back on the fertility horse and start again.

After a few additional days of mourning, I snapped out of it and began focusing on when I could do another procedure. In such a short amount of time, things had changed so drastically. Until a few days before, I had been waiting to find out the sex of my baby; now I was waiting to have a miscarriage. The doctor called and said that she was very sorry for me, but she remained encouraged that I had gotten pregnant. It meant that my body could conceive, and to her that was half the battle. She offered words of consolation and then quickly wanted to discuss what was to come over the next week or so.

She explained that my body needed to get rid of the pregnancy, but if this did not happen naturally after a week, they would give me a drug called Methotrexate, which attacks rapidly growing cells and would speed up the hideous process. If nothing happened after the first shot, then another shot could be administered. Once again I thought of my father. Dad had taken the same type of medicine to kill his cancer, which, like a fetus, also consists of rapidly growing cells.

After a week, nothing had happened, so I went in to get the shot. It was quick and painless, and I had no reaction whatsoever.

Another week passed, during which Christmas came and went with little celebration. My body, still thinking it was pregnant, continued holding on tightly to the pregnancy. I was able to make a weak joke that it was just like me to be tenacious. What was once considered a positive attribute had become a liability. I was going to be forced to go in for another dose. The day before shot number two, I went out for a little retail therapy. While in a trendy store, I was marveling at how expensive the thongs were when I began to get cold and disoriented. The saleslady got me a cup of water and kept

saying, "Oh! Maybe you're pregnant." I mumbled that it was probably just the overpriced thongs. I rushed out of the store, weakly got
into my car, and called Chris as I drove home. I told him not to
leave work, but he insisted.

The moment I got into the house, I started writhing in pain.
There was a slow stabbing sensation that came in waves that I imagine
were contractions. What followed were the most excruciating six
hours I have ever experienced. I called my doctor between the surges
of pain, and she said that every two hours I could take the painkiller
Vicodin, though I wasn't to exceed four doses. After hours of hell and
three doses, I was still feeling no relief. Dr. Vargyas said if it got unbearable, I could go to the hospital, where they would give me mor-
phine. I didn't want to leave my house. Chris had been begging to
take me to the hospital ever since he got home, but I felt I wouldn't be
doing anything differently there than I would at home, and I couldn't
handle all the prying tabloid eyes. What was happening was obviously
my body's way of dealing with the situation, and I had to defer to it.
The scar tissue had no elasticity, so this miscarriage was even more
painful than most. I wasn't trying to be a hero and had to believe the
Vicodin would eventually help. The pain, and the whole scenario, felt
almost primitive, but I knew I had no choice but to endure it.

Chris stayed within earshot, and our dog lay at the foot of the
bed with her chin resting on my feet. At one point, crouching very
low, she actually crawled up to lick my cheek before returning to her
former position. She felt my sadness and instinctively understood
the extent of my pain. Chris would've licked my face, too, if he
thought it would help. I was in the process of losing a child, and all
I could do was wait it out. How disheartening it was to be going

through labor without the hope of a positive outcome. The pain would surely be easier to endure with the prize of a child waiting for me. I stayed in my bed, alone, and knew there wasn't anything anyone could do to make it better.

By eleven-thirty that night, I had taken the fourth dose of medicine and told Chris the pain was getting unbearable and that if I didn't get sleepy in the next thirty minutes, he could take me to the emergency room. I had been moaning and wringing the bedsheets in debilitating pain and had lost a great deal of blood. Chris could do nothing but listen from the other room or come in periodically to stroke my head. He felt helpless, and I saw the relief register in his eyes at the prospect of getting professional help. The contractions were overpowering, and I had already endured six hours of torture. Miraculously, I began to get sleepy. You would think that after consuming enough Vicodin to take down an elephant I would've been knocked out cold, but the pain acted like caffeine injections.

Finally I was so physically and emotionally depleted that I fell asleep. I awoke six hours later, exhausted but no longer in pain. The storm had passed and I had weathered it. I didn't feel any self-pity but instead as if I had gone through a terrible rite of passage. I had never endured such a lonely and painful experience; it had aged and matured me. I concluded that I had lost an innocence seen only in people who have yet to be deeply disappointed by life. As I mourned the loss of my baby, I also quietly said goodbye to a certain naïveté that I once had, that things would always turn out just fine.

Chris took me to my doctor's office, and I gave Dr. Vargyas the details of my nightmare. She did a sonogram and there it was: What was once a chamber infused with life was now a dark cavern. I had gotten so used to seeing "the little cashew," as I referred to the fetus. Now my uterus looked like a robbed safe. I was crying but still wanted to discuss our options for moving forward as soon as possible.

Though we tried to stay focused on what our next move would be, we still had to tell the rest of our families and close friends about the miscarriage. Knowing that we'd soon begin the treatments again didn't make this any easier, but it had to be done. We had learned a valuable lesson, however, and decided that next time we would wait to tell people until the pregnancy was further along. The press, thank God, wasn't privy to this pregnancy until later, so at least I didn't have to deal with them as well. Everybody we knew reacted differently, but my dad seemed the most upset. It could be that he had a sense of his own time line and felt the urgency of each passing month. I reassured him that because I had gotten pregnant before, I could do so again, and we should consider this a positive sign. He would meet his grandchild.

One positive aspect of the miscarriage was that it caused my cervix to open, thereby increasing the number of fertility options available to us. For the next seven months, life became an interminable series of fertility treatments: artificial inseminations, a Clomid cycle, in vitro with fresh, fertilized eggs. After each of these procedures failed, my doctor reminded us that I had gotten pregnant before and that I shouldn't lose hope. The key was to continue.

Although she tried to console me, she couldn't offer an explanation as to why none of these procedures had worked. Chris and I were starting to feel desperate and like something was very wrong. The doctors had never seen someone like me not get pregnant. Come to think of it, during this entire process, we kept on hearing the same thing. They had never seen anything quite like this; my cervix was unique; bypassing it should have worked but didn't; my miscarriage was incredible, etc. Nothing I had experienced was considered common. Why couldn't I be common? Everyone around me was getting pregnant. I was starting to feel bitter. Maybe I really wasn't meant to have kids. Catholic guilt began creeping in again, as did resentment. I didn't want to hear about how *unique* I was. I didn't want to be happy anymore for the many other people who were having kids. I knew that their blessing had nothing to do with me, but it felt like a slap in the face. I wasn't yet open to adoption. I wanted to be pregnant, and it didn't seem like too much to ask! I didn't want to feel guilty about wanting my own child. Why wasn't I getting pregnant? What was wrong with me? Chris believed it would eventually happen, but I was losing faith, not to mention stamina. I became almost grim and lost much of my humor. The first time I got pregnant had obviously been a fluke, a tease, a nasty trick played on me by Mother Nature.

Slowly people stopped asking about how the fertility treatments were going. I never had positive news, so they wouldn't bring it up. Some people whom I didn't know well or hadn't seen in a while would ask how the baby was, assuming I'd already had the first one. I wouldn't get invited to baby showers because friends thought it would be too painful. People avoided telling me their good news. I was beginning to feel like a freak. I found comfort with other people who had fertility issues, but the bottom line was that we all felt pretty alone. What continued was an inordinate amount of unsolicited advice. If one more person told me to *relax* or reminded me of how many poor babies needed to be adopted, I was going to *scream*. I searched my heart for altruism but couldn't find any. On top of it all, I hadn't worked in almost a year because my sole focus had been on getting pregnant. I felt like I was missing out on opportunities and had nothing to show for it. I had no work and no baby!

It was now midsummer 2002, and I was about ready to call it quits. I was growing weary of the anticipation and the pressure, and Chris said he wasn't sure he could handle seeing me rip off another estrogen patch in frustration. I was recovering from the latest failed attempt to get pregnant, and it wouldn't be long before my system could handle another in vitro procedure. At wit's end, we decided to try one more time. When it didn't work (I knew it wasn't going to), we would take a hiatus from the baby-making and then begin all over again. I might even decide to take a job in between.

At the end of August, the remaining embryos were thawed. Four survived. Dr. Vargyas put them in the transfer catheter and positioned herself at my feet. My temperamental cervix was beginning to act up yet again. As my feet rested in the oven-mitt-covered stirrups, the doctor, in an exasperated tone, declared, "Oh, if I just had another set of hands . . ." To which Chris immediately replied, "If I had a dime for every time I said that when I was down there!" Everyone laughed. We looked at each other as if to say, "Here goes nothing."

I left the hospital and figured this last time I would stay in bed for five straight days, almost twice as long as I needed to. What did

I have to lose? Why not end this process having made every conceivable effort? I laugh now at my choice of words, but it felt like it would be worth a try. I wanted to give myself the benefit of every doubt. If it did not work this time, I would have made sure I had done everything in my power so I would not blame myself for the failure once again. For five straight days, I stayed in my bed and organized snapshots. I went through hundreds of photos and put them all in albums. You know those boxes of pictures you always tell yourself you'll go through on a rainy day? I had boxes of them, and even though I was in sunny California, I pretended it was pouring rain outside. My friends thought I was being extreme, but it kept me occupied and took my mind off of whether I was pregnant or not. It seemed like a perfect way to end a phase in my life.

After this period of bed rest, Chris and I decided to take a trip. I didn't need to get the pregnancy blood test done in L.A., so Chris and I went back to New York to have some overdue fun. We had been so serious for such a long time, we really needed a break. It was almost a weird relief, believing I was not pregnant, because I wanted to wipe the slate clean and start fresh. Playing in our home city was a great way to do just that. It was as if we were being released from jail. On the night before the pregnancy test, Chris and I met up with some old friends and ate and drank to our hearts' content. It was great to be back home in Manhattan and out on the town. Even though I had promised myself I wouldn't have a drink until I took the blood test, I was so convinced I wasn't pregnant that I threw caution to the wind. Somehow in my mind I made a decision to be self-destructive. I figured I had nothing to lose and, not totally clear about whom I was punishing, went on a bit of a rampage. At about two A.M. I informed Chris that I was done for the night. We were about to close a bar called Fannelli's, and even though the news was sure to be bad, I would still have to get up very early in the morning and go to the office of my New York fertility doctor and get the dreaded blood test. I told my husband that no matter how he was feeling the next day, at seven-thirty A.M. we were going uptown to get some more bad news. I could have let him sleep in and gone myself, but I wasn't in the mood to be that generous. Plus, I was pretending not to care but knew I would probably have a real breakdown once I got the results. I was afraid to be alone. We headed back to our little midtown apartment to get a few hours of sleep.

Even at such an early hour, the clinic's waiting room was already unbelievably hot, and Chris was looking and feeling pretty bad. I was just about to find out that I wasn't pregnant for the umpteenth time, so, I admit, he was not getting a great deal of sympathy from me. After my blood was drawn, we discussed how we were going to proceed following the inevitable bad news. The doctor agreed that taking a break from the baby-making was a good idea. I sat in the hot office hearing the drone of the fan and knew I was not pregnant. I just wanted to forget the whole thing for a while.

We went back to our apartment to wait for the call. Chris fell into a hangover-induced sleep, and I started reversing the effects of the night before by consuming a large bottle of water and some carbohydrates.

. . .

SUDDENLY THE PHONE rang. The doctor was on the other end. "Well, the test came back positive. You're pregnant!"

I thought I must be experiencing some dehydrated delirium. I think he went on to give me some details, but I couldn't focus on what was being said and felt like I was a member of the *Peanuts* gang listening to the teacher speaking: "Wah wah wah" was all I could make out. I asked the doctor if he wouldn't mind repeating what he had just said to my husband, because I was having trouble understanding him. I jumped on the bed and nudged Chris to take the phone. My husband, who had just been startled out of slumber, listened to the doctor. He raised his eyebrows, looked at me, said, "Thank you," and hung up.

We stared at each other in disbelief. We were both speechless. I instantly regretted the night before and frantically called the doctor back so he could reassure me that my child wouldn't have fetal alcohol syndrome. The doctor assured me the baby would be fine and that I could also take a flight back to Los Angeles as scheduled. Chris and I were in shock and too scared to celebrate. We remembered what had happened the last time we rejoiced, and tried not to get too excited.

Although outwardly reserved, inside I was screaming. We were thrilled to be pregnant at last, but the fear of another loss was weighing heavily on our minds. Chris held me tight and told me we should try not to worry. We decided that we didn't want to let fear dominate the excitement, and if something bad were to happen, we would deal with it then. For now we would be happy, and

Chris would continue his much needed nap. Pacing back and forth around our small apartment, I excitedly began making plans. A girl? A boy? Blue room, pink, or a safe yellow? Showers, maternity clothes! Books to buy! A healthy eating plan!

I was PREGNANT. I was finally, really PREGNANT!

CHAPTER 2

FASTEN YOUR
SEAT BELTS . . .

AFTER YEARS OF PREPARATION to have a child, I believed I was going to get my wish. Initially we kept the good news to ourselves, but as my belly grew, so did our excitement, and eventually we told our families and friends. It felt wonderful to be pregnant, and I made sure to wear clothes that left nothing to the imagination. Once I started to show, I chose stretchy dresses and any tops that accentuated the eagerly awaited "bump." My favorite outfit was a lightweight black dress that I wore with tall black boots. It became my uniform, and I sometimes even wore the dress over pregnancy jeans with flip-flops. I felt more comfortable dressing my pregnant body than I had when I didn't have a Volkswagen strapped to my stomach.

I loved being pregnant and got a kick out of everything that came with it. I enjoyed eating more, going to yoga regularly, registering at my favorite stores, and trying to pick out names for boys and girls. Each trip to the doctor confirmed that our "little cashew" was developing just fine. I was working with doctors on both coasts so that, wherever I was, I could have all of the early, noninvasive screening tests done at the appropriate times. When it was time to consider amniocentesis, our New York doctor didn't feel it was necessary because the chances of the baby being born with Down syndrome or any other issue had been determined to be very slim. We thought long and hard and then decided that it would give us true peace of mind to know everything was fine. I wanted to be fully informed, so we chose to go ahead and have the test. My doctor, Dr. Rebarber, said it would be more private and quiet for me to do it in a facility outside of the city, so we drove about forty-five minutes to a beautiful New Jersey hospital surrounded by trees. The funny thing was that the doctor had forgotten there was going to be a Christmas party that very day; there were no other appointments scheduled. We walked in the back door (to ensure privacy), and as we got off the elevator, we heard music and laughter. Chris and I cracked up, looked at the doctor, and said, "Real quiet and private, huh?" We all laughed, and the doctor led us to the room where the procedure would be done. I got on the table, saw the size of the needle, and felt a bit sick to my stomach. It was huge! Too late now . . .

With the muffled sounds of the party in the background, the doctor said, "You're going to feel a little prick and then a contraction." Anyone who tells you that amnio doesn't hurt has either blocked it out or is lying. The contraction was painful and it scared me, but there was no more pain after that. It was so weird to see the baby on the monitor, along with a huge needle inserted in the center of my body. What freaked me out was how long the needle stayed in and how deep it went. The baby's arms were moving all around, and the needle was right in front of the baby's body. It looked as if the baby were conducting an orchestra. After we finished, I was advised to have a glass of red wine and a nap (no argument here!). When I got the news that everything was fine and it was a girl, I cried with joy and relief.

GIVEN WHAT WE had gone through to conceive, it was such a comfort to know we had gotten this far and everything was fine. In stark contrast to the prior tumultuous months, I had a surprisingly uneventful pregnancy. Except for swollen feet and ankles and rather severe carpal tunnel syndrome toward the end of my third trimester, I was a calm, happy, waddling pregnant lady. The night before I went into labor, I went to a cocktail party to celebrate the pickup of Chris's show, *I'm with HER*. He created and wrote this sitcom for ABC, and the announcement of the new fall lineup had just been made. Announcement week is basically like frat week for Hollywood, during which all of the producers, writers, and actors invade New York City. It's always a raucous affair, but especially crazy and fun if you've received good news.

I had been told that spicy foods bring on labor and, for some reason, I had been craving spicy broccoli rabe, so I had indulged before going out. At the party, I was in a great mood but soon got tired, so I bowed out of the next stop on the party circuit. I was proud of Chris and felt bad that I was abandoning him, but told him he should go on without me and have a really good time. I joked that he should keep his phone on in case I went into labor. He took me home and ventured back out soon after. I was in bed reading and the baby was doing somersaults (obviously loving the spicy food). It looked like a modern dance number where the bodies move under a sheet and all you see is the occasional limb popping up. I'd see a body part move from one side of my tummy to the other. I wished Chris were there to see it. We had seen her move around before but not to this extent. I'd been told she was breach until the very end, so maybe what I was seeing was her getting into position for the birth. After laughing out loud at her antics, I fell asleep and only briefly woke when Chris returned somewhere around four A.M.

At about seven, I got up to use the bathroom and thought I had finished. But when I stood up, my legs were continuing to get wet. I called out to Chris that I thought my water had broken. I told him to read "the book" (one of the pregnancy tomes I kept by our bed) and see what we were supposed to do next. He quickly yelled out that we should go back to sleep and call the doctor around nine. I thought, Okay, and returned to bed and put a big towel down just in case. It didn't occur to me that this was Chris's own sleepy interpretation of what to do next.

Following what seemed like the best two hours of sleep I had ever had, I got up. The "faucet" had stopped and I felt great. I looked out the window and saw the kind of beautiful New York morning that, when I'm not working, would be the kind of day when I would get a cup of coffee and a bagel from the corner deli and head up to Central Park with the paper. I thought I might do that, but first I called my stepsister Diana to tell her what had happened.

She told me I was "*going nowhere but the hospital!*" She said that I never should have gone back to sleep because of the possibility of infection. I thought I had read everything about labor but didn't recall anyone saying that there was a risk of infection once the water broke. All I remembered was something about a twenty-four-hour window and contractions; I knew to call the doctor when I felt a contraction. We had discussed my water breaking, but given the history with my cervix, we didn't think it would happen. I wasn't having contractions of any kind, so it had never occurred to me to go to the hospital. Even though Diana did make me feel concerned, I felt fine and wasn't in any pain. My mommy friends had all been sent home after going into labor, so I was sure the same would happen to me. I phoned the doctor, and he said to come right away. In the cab, I nervously asked Chris if he thought it was a bad thing that we didn't leave when my water broke. He sheepishly said, "No, but it will be if you have the baby in this cab." He then admitted that he had never looked at the book! At that point I still wasn't in any pain, and all I could do was roll my eyes. Needless to say, I was not sent home.

After enduring twenty-four long hours of labor and being shot up with antibiotics, Pitocin, and an epidural medicine, I had dilated only three centimeters. Dr. Rebarber gently told me that it was time for him to go in and get the baby. I was so tired at that point, it was a relief to know something was going to happen. I thought, Hey, I don't need to be a hero, and honestly didn't feel I'd be able to push anything out of anywhere.

After getting the call that I had gone into labor, Chris's mom and dad had driven all the way from Georgia and were now waiting anxiously in the corridor. This baby was going to be their first grandchild and the first for my mom as well. The day represented the culmination of a lot of hard work, many prayers, and a collective desire. My mother, who had arrived at the hospital practically before we did, already seemed to be in shock. Her face was paler than I had ever seen it, and she kept covering her mouth with her hand. She looked like she was going to either throw up or cry. She said almost nothing and kept moving her right hand from her mouth to her lap, where she would wring it with the left one. It was as if she had endured the labor with me and didn't know what was happening or whether I was really all right.

Chris's parents were quite concerned, too. They're both trained nurses and understood what a physical strain the baby and I were under. They were pacing the hallway discussing my situation. The one person missing was my father, who had tragically passed away just three weeks prior. I lay on the hospital bed wishing he would lumber through the doors, having come directly from the airport, and make me laugh. His presence would've lightened the mood a lot. He was a tall man (six feet seven), with an imposing presence, and was always making jokes. He hated hospitals and dealt with uncomfortable situations by being the life of the party. He would have said something along the lines of "Open her up and get the little monkey out, but put a zipper there in case Brookie wants to have another one!"

The whole family had been invested in this baby, and everyone had hoped I would be able to deliver naturally. Dr. Rebarber had talked to us about the possibility of a C-section, but after a relatively easy nine months, I believed I might not need one. I had in fact dilated for the miscarriage, so it made sense that my "special" cervix might finally behave properly. It never occurred to me that I'd have any more difficulty, and because my water had broken, it now seemed like everything would progress normally. The grandparents were sorry that I wouldn't be able to push the baby out on my own, like I had hoped, because now I would need what was considered a serious operation. They were relieved, however, that the decision had been made. Everyone had been waiting for hours, and we were all exhausted. Suddenly I was being wheeled out for what was turning into an emergency procedure. As I came out of my hospital room on the gurney, I saw the scared look in everyone's eyes. I sensed the disappointment and concern in their expressions and wanted to put them at ease. Used to being the one in control and onstage, I felt compelled to be calm and courteous to the waiting well-wishers.

For my own peace of mind, I began repeating to myself, "Remember this moment." As a proficient multitasker, I knew that my focus could quickly shift from one thing to another; in the process, I sometimes lose the experience of truly being present. So even though my mind was racing, and I was trying to comfort everyone else, I wanted to be as present as possible for this frightening yet momentous occasion.

Someone was filming with a video camera, and I heard a voice say, "Here she comes," as if I were Miss America. I smiled at the absurdity of the comparison. I was lying unnecessarily flat on my back, and I wondered why the doctors didn't let me sit up, at least until I got to the operating room. It was a strange sensation—being the only one who was horizontal and viewing the world upside down and sideways. All at once I felt physically and emotionally distant. It was as if I were floating above the scene and watching everything happen to someone else. (So much for remaining present.) This sensation must be a self-defense mechanism designed to soften the fear of going into surgery. I tried hard not to worry about the fact that, as a result of the epidural, I had no feeling in my legs. I felt separate from everyone and wondered if anyone else sensed this, or if it would just be obvious to me as I watched my face on the video later.

My mother-in-law came up to my head to give me a supportive kiss. Then it was my mother's turn. As she leaned down, I felt uncharacteristically awkward kissing her at that moment. She was my "mommy," and if I gave in to her affection, I might lose my composure. I needed to stay strong. Maybe it was because I was being rolled in to have a baby of my own that I felt strange being the baby with my mother. Whatever the reason, I was uncomfortable receiving her affection. This felt sad to me for some reason, and I immediately tried to reconcile it in my mind. Out of habit, I pretended I was in a movie and this scene represented the symbolic rite of passage from child to adult/mother. I often did these types of visualizations as a kid, especially in fearful situations, and it usually calmed me down or made things seem less threatening. Whether this current situation was a rite of passage or not, the truth was that both mothers were clearly shaken, and I felt it was up to me to make them feel better. I reassured everyone that I wasn't at all concerned or scared and that a C-section had always been a possibility (even though I hadn't really expected it). We all remembered the tale about my being "cervically challenged," didn't we? I added that I was lucky I had even dilated as much as I did and that it would all be fine. Inside I was crushed.

"Look at it this way," I said. "Don't you want to meet the little cashew sooner rather than later?"

I accepted the rest of their kisses and blessings and smiled. With mounting anxiety I began searching for my husband's face. I needed to tell him that I was not fine and couldn't ever go through any of this again!

I couldn't see him because everything was whizzing by me upside down, and the gurney, it seemed, was being pushed faster and faster. Soon I was being wheeled through big metal doors, down a long hallway, and all I saw were passing bright fluorescent lights, blurred walls, and my huge stomach blocking my massively swollen Flintstone feet. A week earlier, a girlfriend had taken a picture of my feet in flip-flops—for months, they had been the only shoes I could wear. She didn't show me the photo for almost a year, because she feared the sight of my Miss Piggy feet would send me into a tailspin. I can laugh now, but she was right in thinking that I wouldn't have found it too funny earlier.

Chris's face appeared. He was running alongside the gurney. He reassured me that I wouldn't have to do any of this ever again if I didn't want to, especially wear the flattering light blue paper shower cap! I smiled, and just the sight of his face peeking out from under his matching cap calmed me enough that I felt ready to face what was coming up.

I had always hoped I would have a husband I could rely on, and with whom I could be completely myself at all times. (I'm sure he wishes I weren't so uncensored, but as of yet I haven't scared him off.) Chris is that person, and I am blessed daily to have him in my life. Without him, I am sure I wouldn't have survived any of this.

Chris was getting prepped to be in the delivery room, and the grandparents had all receded. The only people with me in the delivery room were Chris and my oldest friend, Lyda, who had just arrived and was also getting prepped. Everything turned very serious, and I got quiet as we entered the cold, sterile room filled with masked nurses. My doctor obviously remembered our countless conversations about my strong desire to deliver vaginally. Over the past few months, he had begun to believe we would both get our wish of natural childbirth. I could tell he didn't want to have to cut me open. He had been so encouraging during labor, and he, too, had thought that since I dilated the three centimeters, I would have continued doing so and been able to deliver naturally. He felt sorry that such a long labor would result in a C-section. Being sensitive to my disappointment, he appeared over me to reiterate, "C-sections don't carry any less merit than vaginal births." For some reason, it made me giggle inside every time I heard this accomplished doctor say the word "vaginal." I kept thinking of Beavis and Butt-head: "Vaginal, heh, heh."

Being polite, I thanked him for his encouragement. I was trying not to feel overwhelmed by the fact that what was about to happen was major surgery and was the antithesis of the image of childbirth to which I had become quite attached over the years. It did seem, however, like a fitting last stage to my unconventional and extremely difficult journey. The dream I had of pushing and sweating, and being rewarded by seeing my child born and placed on my chest even before the cord was cut, was not going to happen. The alternative, which was to be cut wide open, was hardly appealing, but I did want my daughter out of me alive and healthy. I tried to tell myself that having a C-section would be easier than more hours of discomfort or labor. I was depleted of practically all of my energy and was impatient to have my baby. For the whole exhausting twenty-four hours, I kept focusing on the thrilling fact that I was actually going to have a child. This thought helped me to endure the arduous process.

After we were all in the freezing room, I was transferred to the operating table. I managed to muster what would be my last attempt at humor by telling the male nurses not to grunt so loudly as they heaved my bloated body. Once I was on the table, a big blue sheet was put up; it acted as a curtain, blocking the upper half of my body from the lower. This way I couldn't see the surgery. My arms were positioned out from my shoulders, forming a big T. I quickly made it clear that I didn't want to be strapped down. I promised not to move my arms or to reach over the curtain and strangle the man in the doctor outfit who was firing up the chain saw.

I smelled something burning and, fearing an electrical short and potential loss of power, asked what it was. Before anyone could answer, Chris exclaimed that a nurse was making toast. Being momentarily brain-dead and quite vulnerable, I thought it might be true, based on the proximity of the cafeteria. The incision for the C-section had evidently been made and was being cauterized. Once I put two and two together, I felt like throwing up. I pictured the scene in *Alien* when the guy's chest opens up and the creature comes out. There is the sound of the man's flesh ripping and the slimy creature popping out, squealing. Ugh! The doctor peeked over the top of the curtain and told me not to worry. He had cut beneath the cute little tattoo I impulsively got one day at my bikini line. I thanked him and tried to shake off the images of seared flesh and aliens that were now imprinted on my brain.

The same man who, up until this moment, had been nothing but nurturing was now using all of his weight to crush my abdomen. I saw his head and shoulders rise above the blue divider and then disappear, and I felt a tremendous weight on my body. It looked like he was a WWE wrestler pile-driving into my stomach. I felt hard-core tugging and pulling and pouncing, and I couldn't believe the force being exerted. (What ever happened to the beauty of childbirth?)

In the room there was a big window overlooking the East River. This was the same river that I drove along every day as a little girl on my way to school, the same river that served as the burial place of my first and only turtle, and the same river where my husband and I would wave frantically at boats passing by, trying to get a reaction from the people onboard. I looked at the sun reflecting off of the water and never thought I would find myself looking at the river from this point of view. I was bombarded by childhood memories. My mind drifted, and I temporarily forgot what was happening. It was odd that my mind could drift while this guy was pounding on my stomach, but I guess it served as a diversion to keep me from thinking about what was actually going on.

I was jolted out of my reverie when I heard the words "Cord wrapped, cord wrapped!" Another doctor had been called in to assist. My hearing got muffled, and not only could I not hear the James Taylor CD I had chosen to listen to during delivery, but I started to feel faint. I took deep yoga breaths so as not to panic. I began to think that in a spiritual sense, maybe this was the real reason for the C-section. Had I been pushing, my baby might have been strangled by the umbilical cord, which we found out was wrapped around her neck and body three times. I turned my head once again and, focusing on the peaceful water, began to pray. I prayed that my little girl would be safe. I prayed that she had not been hurt or had her health compromised because of the wrapped cord. The air in the room seemed to shift. Earlier it had been so cold; now it was very hot and thick. The doctors' concentration was palpable. I moved my head from side to side and looked around the room, trying to ascertain my situation. I could see only furrowed brows and focused eyes glaring over surgical masks. I could tell there was sweat beneath those masks.

The two specialists were working in silent tandem. I wanted to scream, "What is happening, tell me, tell me, tell me!" but I remained quiet. I wished I were a mind reader. Just as my thoughts turned even darker, James Taylor came to my rescue. His voice became slightly audible again, and to keep my fear at bay, I focused on that and on the grip of my husband's warm hand. After what felt like hours in this position but what was, in reality, probably only a few minutes, I heard the sound I had been praying for. At the same moment that the lyric "How sweet it is to be loved by you" filled the room, I heard my daughter. That strong voice—somewhere between a squawk and a bark—belonged to the little creature who had been living inside my body for the last nine months. It seemed to be telling me that she had arrived and was okay.

Rowan had been born, and a nurse read her statistics out loud. She was 7 pounds, 5 ounces, and 21 inches long. The doctor lifted her over the curtain so I could see her, and I cried. They were tears of relief. I couldn't believe she was really my baby. She looked nothing like me. Nonetheless, the mere sight of her took my breath away. Just moments before, she had been hidden in me, and now she

existed in this world. It was too incredible to grasp. She was my little girl! She looked strong and perfect and had an extremely judgmental expression on her round, red face. Lyda said, "Look at her
expression! She looks so unimpressed!" The baby actually did have
a scowl on her face as she opened her eyes and, with a disapprov-
ing and critical expression, seemed to be saying, "I went through
all that for this? You have got to be kidding me." She was swaddled
and handed directly to her father. Since I had been gutted like a
fish and was still in the crucifix position, I couldn't even hold my
own baby, but instead had to be satisfied with smelling her warm
cheek.

In addition, my uterus, which they discovered had herniated,
was now sitting above the incision on my belly and was being examined by my doctor. (It's shocking but true that the uterus can be
taken out, manipulated in this way, and then put back in the body.)
He peered over the blue wall that was still hiding the war zone that
was my body and asked if I remembered any doctor ever saying anything about a weakness in my uterus. At that point I was lucky to
even know what a uterus was, but, ever the people pleaser, I wanted
to provide a helpful answer. I struggled to recount any details about
my anatomy that could be important. Now I really felt faint. I finally
recalled something about the lining of my uterus being thick
enough for implantation, but as I struggled to garner enough energy
to explain this, he had already disregarded my babble and returned
to the scene of the crime. I was now either going to throw up or pass
out and proceeded to ask a nurse if one was, in fact, preferable for a
person in my current position. Her response was to put an alcohol
pad under my nose. The smell was surprisingly delightful. I didn't

throw up or faint, but I probably should have, because things quickly turned even graver.

The room got very quiet, and I felt another shift taking place. The baby was carried away to be checked, and Chris followed her. Although I was feeling scared, I still didn't want my baby out of her dad's sight. Happiness and promise now out of the room, the doctor got down to the business of telling me what was happening. He came around the curtain and pulled up a stool. Sliding closer to me and stopping level with my head, he explained that the herniated area of my uterus was inhibiting the muscle from contracting back to normal, and as a result, I kept losing blood. He wouldn't do a transfusion just yet, but if I kept on bleeding, he might have to perform a hysterectomy. Let's see: hysterectomy, blood transfusion? What next? My head started to spin, but all I could do was listen. I started to panic and prayed the doctor would stay conservative and not make any rash decisions. I had to trust him. I was the one looking like roadkill. I understood instantly why the words "hysterectomy" and "hysteria" have the same root. I fought to remain calm but was losing.

I asked, "Am I going to die?"

"If it's your uterus or your life, we know which one to take, but I feel confident enough to put your uterus back in and watch you for forty-eight hours."

What a choice! I wanted both!

In a state of shock, I calmly kept repeating, "Okay," but I felt a certain panic mounting. Was that it? Had I fulfilled my purpose here, and in life? Was I purely a vessel, a pod, and now I was no longer necessary? Was my reference to *Alien* accurate? In an attempt to make sense of my situation, I tried to assess the facts I knew for sure. My baby was healthy, and that was what I had prayed for. Maybe I should have been more specific about what I wanted — like, I don't know, that I wanted to live and keep my organs!

Instead of celebrating new life, I found myself in a fight for my own. I was continuing to lose a great deal of blood, and though there seemed to be no distress in the doctor's voice, I feared I was dying. The doctor had done everything he could to stop the bleeding. We would have to wait and see if any of it had worked or if he would have to bring me back in for an emergency hysterectomy. I was prepared for none of this. I thought I'd have my baby, get stitched up, and all would be fine. How did this happen? And why? Hadn't it all been hard enough? Having another baby was hardly appealing at this point, but I still would have preferred to stay alive and, greedy or not, keep everything I came in with. Later my husband would say that, although he was very concerned about my health, he knew I wasn't in danger of dying and was confident that the doctors had it all under control. That's probably true, but at the moment I didn't know that, and Chris wasn't the one with his guts spread out like a garage sale.

How fleeting was the joy provided by hearing my daughter's voice. Fittingly, the CD was finished. I was terrified and angry and couldn't understand how the bliss had disappeared so quickly. I had been so overjoyed to hear her cry, and my heart had soared at the sight of her little body. The miracle had occurred, and as quickly as the delight had arrived, so it had been taken away. I envisioned a glorious uniting with my newborn. She had grown inside of me, and we had lived as one person and without seeing each other for so long. How beautiful that meeting would be! I had always imagined that birth would be the closest thing to grace I'd ever experience, yet in reality there was nothing graceful about it.

My mind whirling, I glanced up to see my husband, who had since returned and who I assumed had been informed about my predicament. He was holding our little girl, who had been swaddled like a burrito. She was wide-eyed and serious and appeared to understand everything that was happening.

Although slightly in shock and definitely exhausted, Chris looked optimistic and peaceful. Well, wasn't he lucky! I was bleeding buckets, and he was holding on tightly to a perfect frowning angel baby. I stared at this glowing father/child image and was bombarded with feelings of jealousy, fear, and rage. I wanted to be in his position right now. After all I went through to get here, was this my reward? I did all the work and yet felt like I wasn't being permitted to enjoy any of it. I don't think I've ever been that scared. As I witnessed life continuing all around me, the survival instinct surged through my body, and I thought, Oh my God, I don't want to die. I am not ready to die. I want to live! I felt angry that the people around me were all up and very well. I heard a voice in my head that said, "They can't help you. You have to stay alive." It was a strange reaction, but I didn't care about anything else except recovering and avoiding any more traumas. I was on a mission to keep my body intact. The baby was fine, so I could concentrate on me.

The doctor put all of my plumbing back where it should be. As the layers of stitches were being configured, he informed me that they were being done in such a way as to create a frown from my point of view but a smile from his. First of all, I was in no mood for humor, and more important, my "frown" was becoming a full-blown, seething snarl. I remained quiet and would be told later that I appeared remarkably calm. I am an actress, after all. And I had no choice but to stay still. Jumping off the table and joining my turtle in the East River really wasn't an option, but it sure was an image that strongly appealed to me. I figured I'd just wait. The team finished assembling me, and it was time to get wheeled back to the waiting loved ones.

Rowan had preceded me and was a hit. The family was already calling her by her full name. We had chosen it months ago, and although we loved the name, it sounded strange to hear it out loud. I began wondering if we had made the right choice. "Rowan" is a Gaelic word meaning "little red one." Rowan's small bit of hair had a reddish hue to it, but for us this was pure coincidence. We chose the name because we loved the sound of Irish names and there was folklore surrounding it. It was the name of a huge red oak tree whose roots went deep. Apparently, Robin Hood's sister was also named Rowan, and she was similarly altruistic. In addition, Rowan Mayfair, the heroine in Anne Rice's *The Witching Hour,* is one of my favorite characters in any book. I have heard many people say that they had a few choices of names for their baby and that, from the moment the child came out, the newborn looked more like one of the names than any of the others. Rowan didn't look like any particular name, and I stopped questioning it. Her name was Rowan, and one day it would make more sense to me.

Though I had left the drama of the operating room, I had entered a different kind of mayhem by coming back to my room. Here the real circus began. Some of our close relatives had arrived while we were in surgery and wanted to see their newest relation. They had been told about my physical condition and were torn between fear for me and utter joy at the arrival of the baby. I appeared to be okay, so much of the focus was on Rowan. My godmother had come straight from the airport and had joined the spectacle. People kept entering our room, and between various family members and some close friends, the flow of traffic was almost unreal. I couldn't rest because of the constant stream of well-wishers, not to mention the curious staff. I didn't have the energy to ask people to leave and felt like I would have time to digest it all and relax later. (Relax? Ha! Little did I know.) In addition, Chris was so proud and was animatedly showing off his daughter to everyone; I hated to ruin his happiness. There seemed to be an endless amount of new information to learn with regard to a newborn, and I couldn't understand why most of it hadn't been explained to us during the previous day and a half, when I had been a captive audience. The nurses, each of whom seemed to have the same task to do, all brought with them a different piece of advice. I couldn't tell if they were doing their jobs, were trying to be genuinely helpful, or were just nosy. I figured the more ears that heard the instructions, the better, and I told the extended family that they had better be paying attention.

I was in incredible pain, and the epidural guy got exasperated by my complaining. He was a huge man whose accent sounded like he was from Transylvania. He kept asking me, "On level wan to ten, vat level eez dee payn?" I said it was at a nine.

"Eet kant be true. I hav eet on highest level!"

He seemed so frustrated with me that I started to lie and gave him lower and lower numbers when he checked on me. After four hours of hell, Dr. Rebarber arrived and said I didn't look too good. I asked to speak to him alone and explained the pain had reached beyond an eleven. He made "The Count" check the needle, and we discovered that it was unattached to my body and had been for quite some time. It got reattached, and the pain was soon alleviated.

Later on, the lactation specialist came in and wanted to show me how Rowan needed to adhere to me for breast-feeding. In Los Angeles I had taken a breast-feeding class and had learned about latching on, but apparently, as with rap music, there's an East Coast and a West Coast version, and there's always a battle brewing between the two. This nurse said to disregard how it was done on the West Coast and pay attention to her instructions. She gave the speech about how imperative it was that Rowan breast-feed now, so as to get the colostrum. This bodily fluid is produced by a new mother only right after childbirth, before the regular milk comes in, and it has the antibodies the baby needs to be healthy. The pressure was on to get this stuff into Rowan as quickly as possible or else, I was told, it would dry up. The nurse kept referring to the process of the liquid coming in as letdown. It was an appropriate term for this frustrating process. No matter how my baby got angled, I couldn't seem to position her mouth correctly. I felt like she would be the one who was "let down" if I didn't figure out how to perform this presumably natural process.

Chris tried to help. Not a good idea. He seems to have a way to improve almost any situation, no matter how grave (much to my chagrin, he's usually right), and I almost always defer to his knowledge, but where my breasts are concerned, I draw the line! Between the lactation specialist, the nurse, and my husband, nobody could

get it right, including me. I had no personal feelings about the lactation specialist or the nurses except that they were a bit too much like
flower children about the whole process. I resented how easy and
natural and beautiful they made breast-feeding sound, and I almost
expected to see little birds flying around their heads.

I was becoming even more delirious with fatigue. Nothing had
gone smoothly, nor did it look like it would anytime soon. I felt like
I was somehow not performing up to speed as a woman. My body
was not doing anything I asked of it, and I was starting to think I
would never get the hang of this mothering business. I am a perfec-
tionist and have always been an overachiever with little tolerance for
my shortcomings. Admittedly, this has caused a great deal of stress
in my life and sometimes has made it hard for me to accept things as
they are. I am impatient with myself and have high expectations. I
wanted to breast-feed instantly and with ease. I had always envisioned the experience like this: The baby is on the mother's breast,
the mother's hair is cascading down, and the infant is gazing up with
complete contentment. I see the mother, head tilted, looking into
her baby's eyes with an expression of total peace and relaxation. The
connection is seamless and perfect.

I couldn't seem to give myself a break, but after a few more tries,
Rowan got the hang of it, and I realized she was not going to starve.
It remained extremely difficult to nurse, however, since Rowan had
to wear a sunlamp paddle for jaundice. This slightly stiff felt-and-
plastic paddle included an ultraviolet light that needed to shine on
her body to help get rid of the jaundice. The contraption came with
a long cord that got slipped up the back of anything she was wearing
and had to be plugged into an electrical socket. The whole apparatus

was awkward, and she looked like a Native American baby in an il-luminated papoose. The nurses kept saying, "She must get her bilirubin back down." (At the time all I could think was Who's Billy Rubin?)

In addition, Rowan had been put in a leg and body harness be-cause the balls at the tops of her thighbones weren't fitting properly into the hip sockets. Evidently, when women are pregnant, they secrete a hormone that makes their hips widen for childbirth. Some-times babies, especially girls, react to this hormone in utero and are born with their hip sockets not completely formed. Then the baby has to wear a harness to keep the tops of the thighbones in place un-til the hip sockets develop properly. When the specialist educated me about this condition and about the hormone that spreads a woman's hips, I tried to make light of this additional bad news. It all seemed so terrible that I nervously couldn't resist making a joke. I have always had good-size hips and an ample rear end, so I said, "I must have been producing this hormone all my life." I got only a polite smile out of the less than humorous hip specialist, so I shut up.

The sight of this tiny baby all strapped in a harness and lit up like a Christmas tree was heartbreaking. The white Velcro fastening bands were positioned so that she looked like one of those wooden puppets with a string between its legs and, when you pull it, its knees reach up to its ears. Rowan was harnessed so that she looked like her string was always being pulled. She screamed whenever it was readjusted. The physician swore she was in no pain and that it was usually more uncomfortable for the parents to see their baby in this contraption. I couldn't believe she wasn't bothered by it, but what did I know? The doctor warned us that it made changing diapers tricky. That seemed to be the least of our problems.

Dr. Rebarber came by to tell me that I had stopped the more severe bleeding that he had spoken of during the surgery. He had watched my progress closely, and it appeared that my uterus was, in fact, contracting back to normal. He'd still need to watch me a bit longer but felt confident about my being able to keep all my parts in their places. He added that I would even be able to carry another child if I wanted to. Whoa, baby! This was not high on my list of priorities at the moment. I was relieved to know that I could keep my uterus and that I didn't have to endure another major surgery, but truthfully, the thought of going through any of this ever again made me shudder.

Chris, who had stopped trying to be a lactation consultant, had become an instant paternal prototype. I watched him navigate the family and, while holding Rowan's swaddled body (which he had swaddled himself), make phone calls to friends. He maneuvered the harness and the diapers as if he'd been doing it all of his life. This was a man who was great with older kids but had always been awkward and stiff around babies, to the point where they could sense it and would start to cry. Out of necessity, he had made a 180-degree turn and had become an even more incredible man in my eyes. Rowan was also a good sport during all the fussing and cried only when she was hungry or needed her diaper changed. The ultraviolet paddle quickly made a difference, and I watched her become less jaundiced the longer it was on her. I was relieved that at least something was going right.

Not even two full days after major surgery, one of the countless nurses who had been telling me what to do came in to wash me. I tried to be nonchalant as this burly woman hooked her arm under my huge knees, lifted up my legs, and, using a squeezable water bottle, bathed me like a baby. It was humiliating and almost unbearable. I couldn't seem to get any of my pride back, and nervous jokes about a bikini wax did nothing to help. Next she told me that I had to walk to the creepy tiled bathroom and make a "movement." You have to be kidding! The place resembled something out of the movie *One Flew Over the Cuckoo's Nest*. There was a metal bar going all around the walls that you could hold on to for support or in case you fell, and a weird fold-down seat in a shower that had no curb and drained into the middle of the room. I couldn't walk without hunching over, and I had stitches all around the very area that contracted during a "movement." I hadn't eaten in days, my stomach muscles had been torn apart, and I was supposed to bear down and have something to show for it? The pain I felt from simply sitting up was almost more than I could stand. The stitches pulled and my uterus ached. I was taking Tylenol, but the stronger pain medicine had worn off. I thought the pain would keep me awake at night, but it was impossible to tell because I was up every hour and a half, feeding the little machine I called my daughter.

Eventually (without being too graphic) I took a little red pill that contributed to success in the lavatory. The burly nurse who looked like Mrs. Doubtfire—but whose manner was reminiscent of Nurse Ratched—congratulated me and promised it would all get easier. I couldn't tell if she was making a poop joke or being metaphysical, but I faked a painful laugh anyway. The whole ordeal was mortifying and depressing.

Chris continually tried to be lighthearted and expressed his usual humor at every opportunity, all the while saying how beautiful Rowan was and how well I was doing. I couldn't join him in his appreciation, and I hardly responded to his efforts. I felt spent and used up and didn't have the energy to pretend any differently. I didn't feel, or act, like my usual positive self. Chris kept holding the baby and talking to her, and it was beautiful to see how easy he was with this tiny being. I was anything but easy with her, but I assumed those feelings would undoubtedly change with time.

Over the five days that I was in the hospital with Rowan, I was in a bizarre state of mind, experiencing feelings that ranged from embarrassment to stoicism to melancholy to shock, practically at once. I didn't feel at all joyful, but I attributed this to being tired and needing to recover physically. The pain was becoming more manageable, and I was walking less hunched over. The doctor said that I would be able to leave soon. Chris traveled back and forth to our apartment to take care of our dog, to shower, or to bring me clothes or whatever else I needed from home. With him gone, I was left alone with this tiny newborn baby. She was in the medical version of a bassinet, with no wicker or lace but only clear plastic and metal, and was rolled right next to my hospital bed. She had lost a bit of weight, which they assured me was normal, and now weighed 7 pounds. She was very alert but a complete stranger to me. Here she was, on her back and with apparatuses all around, and I couldn't seem to recognize her. I had expected, upon seeing her, to feel a sense of déjà vu. Instead I didn't remember her at all. I had always thought there would be an instant bond between us, but no matter how long I stared, I couldn't seem to feel one. I had anticipated knowing her intimately after carrying her around for so long. Now I couldn't even get close enough to feel her skin with my hands—I could fit only a finger under the harness. I kept leaning over and smelling her to see if I could recognize her scent or anything familiar about her. In a strange way, she seemed to know me much better than I did her. She was able to look directly at me, as if she had everything all figured out. I felt self-conscious when alone with her. She seemed pure and honest and raw, and it unsettled me. I tried to talk to her when we were alone.

"Baby girl, please be patient with me. I think I'm having a hard time here, and I don't want you to be sad because of it. Please love me. I promise I'll try to get better."

I whispered these words to her in hopes that they would register in some way. While Chris was out, I kept calling him on his cell phone to ask if he was coming back. I wanted to make sure that neither the trauma we had endured nor my less than jovial personality had sent him running. He continually assured me of his imminent return and of his love for both his wife and baby daughter. I couldn't wait to be at home with Chris and the baby and not have strangers coming into my room every ten minutes. Home sounded more and more like a peaceful refuge.

Our next challenge was to figure out how and when to leave the hospital. Unfortunately, unlike most people, I couldn't just leave the building without being watched. I knew that our departure must be planned and navigated properly, or there would be press hounding us the entire way home. This is one of the most un-nerving aspects of being in the public eye. No matter how resentful I feel about this perpetual intrusion, I always need to remain calm and in charge. People ask me if I ever get used to the loss of privacy. Even though I have had to deal with it since I was a baby myself, the answer is *no*. My strategy has been to try and find ways to be congenial but not completely vulnerable.

With regards to my leaving the hospital, I could at least be phys-ically prepared so that when the inevitable photo was sent out across the wire, I would look my best (all things considered). I remem-bered seeing a photo of Sarah Jessica Parker leaving the hospital and remarking on how chic she looked. Before I left for the hospital, I had laid out a black dress that I knew would fit because I had tried it on when I was hugely pregnant. I chose a short string of pearls that had belonged to my dad's mother. The shoes were another story, but even though I still had Miss Piggy insteps, I managed to complete the outfit with a pair of high-heeled pumps. I had Chris bring my outfit to the hospital; I knew I wouldn't be sorry I went through the trouble when I saw the tabloid photo plastered everywhere and cap-tioned in every language. At least I wouldn't have to deal with the speculation that my delivery was anything less than easy.

If I didn't face the press as I left, they would undoubtedly follow me all the way to my apartment and camp outside until I came out. It would be easier to take Rowan out the front door, let them get their first photo of the baby, and maybe then they'd be satisfied. Exposing my tiny daughter to the paparazzi made me uncomfortable, but I would make it fast and on our terms, and hopefully she wouldn't be affected by the noise. It was daylight, so flashes wouldn't be an issue.

Even though I always try to be as prepared as possible, I also try not to become overly concerned about what other people think and to just do what I want to do. In this case, however, I had to protect my husband and now my baby from prying eyes. I was responsible for thrusting them into the spotlight, and I had to navigate my celebrity in a way that didn't compromise them. This meant sparing them from being stalked by photographers. A documented life is one of the weirdest consequences of celebrity, but when you consider that details about my orthodontist appointments, my first period, and my virginity have all been publicized, you can understand my continual need to be prepared.

Chris had gone to get a decaf Starbucks for me and returned just as I was about to get dressed. I had asked some friends to help with the beautifying process. They were all set up to start, and I was in a robe standing by the window. Before they began, I turned to Chris and had my first breakdown.

"I am so sorry!" I cried.

"What's wrong, what happened?" Chris asked.

"Look at what they have to work with! Look at the size of me!"

I hadn't entered the hospital this bloated and in fact was not even that big after nine months of pregnancy. But because of all of the medicine that I had been pumped with intravenously, I had retained so much fluid that I looked inflated. My fingers were like sausages. I could press my thumb into my calf, and when I removed it, the indentation was still there. I couldn't even cross or hold my legs together because my knees were too enormous. I looked like a cartoon figure and waddled like the Michelin Man. Chris tried to console me. "Honey, you look beautiful. Come on, you just had a baby. I promise you'll feel better soon."

Either he knew he had to say something encouraging, or maybe he was blinded enough by love to believe I didn't look that bad. He convinced me that I wasn't the monster I saw in the mirror and that it would all seem better once I was dressed and heading home. My friends cheerfully shared stories of how ugly they felt when they had their kids, and they began to doll me up. The sound of the blow dryer helped Rowan fall asleep in my arms, and I quietly gave in to their ministrations. After about an hour of good magicians' work, I was ready to put on my outfit and hobble out. We dressed Rowan in a sweet little antique dress, wrapped her in a blanket, and were ready to depart.

At the hospital exit, as expected, we were met by cameras and comments. The photographers asked the baby's name and tried to get a close-up of our five-day-old daughter. I was struck by how much of an intrusion this was. I was accustomed to it, but it felt different where she was concerned. It felt extremely personal and even more invasive. Suddenly I didn't want them to know her name, nor did I want the cameras in her little face. I regretted putting her through this but felt as if I didn't have a choice. A wave of fear washed over me, and I instantly thought something was going to happen to her out here. I sought the refuge of the locked car. Rowan didn't cry once. As I entered the waiting vehicle, a smile frozen on my face, Rowan looked straight up at me as if to say, "Mom, these people are too close." I looked down at her and was taken aback by the directness of her gaze. Once again, she seemed wiser than I felt.

Silently I made a promise to protect her. Sitting safely in the car, with our newborn buckled into her car seat, I peeled the shoes off of my Silly Putty feet and sighed with relief. It was done, and nobody followed us. We were finally on our way home, and I couldn't wait to relax. At that juncture, I had no knowledge of what lay in store for me behind the closed doors of our apartment.

CHAPTER 3

WHY AM I
CRYING MORE
THAN MY BABY?

AS I WALKED BAREFOOT into our apartment, carrying my newborn, I felt disoriented. When I had left this space five days ago, I was a totally different person. Now, passing through the same doors, I had become a mother, and the world, as I related to it, had entirely changed. As I held my five-day-old baby girl in my arms, I looked around the apartment and thought, Where am I? It was like being in the Twilight Zone, and I kept waiting for someone to turn off the TV.

Chris and I were suddenly alone with a brand-new baby, and we weren't sure what to do. We stared at each other for a while and then tried to settle in. I changed into a pair of Chris's shorts, which were the only thing that fit over the girdle I had to wear as a result of the C-section. My legs were far from shorts-worthy, but I tried not to think about that. I was just happy to be out of my dress. We put the little one in a Moses basket. Then, in an attempt to gain control, I decided to unpack immediately and tidy up the house. Chris kindly reminded me that I'd just had a baby and the tidying up could wait. He ordered me to bed and added that once we all got some sleep, I could neaten to my heart's desire. He was under the impression that the baby would drift off into a peaceful slumber and we would all get caught up on the sleep we had been deprived of in the hospital. I must admit that I, too, naively believed that because we were home and away from constant interruptions, rest was imminent. Almost every mother I knew had let her new baby sleep at least one night in the hospital nursery before going home so the mom could launch into baby land slightly rested. Since we were too afraid of the press or even of a staff member sneaking photos of Rowan, we never let her out of our sight. Consequently, neither Chris nor I had really slept in five days, and we were feeling quite beaten up because of it. Unfortunately we soon found out that being home hardly provided the respite we craved.

Chris and I had planned to spend a week alone at home with the baby, just the three of us, before having our families come for a visit. We had wanted uninterrupted time to bond as a family. We chose not to have a baby nurse, either, because not only did we not want a stranger in our home, but we figured we could handle it ourselves until our relatives came to stay. We couldn't have been more wrong. We were anything but peaceful, and because we were alone, we were overwhelmed.

To add to the upheaval of our lives at the time of Rowan's birth, we had moved into a new apartment, at the opposite end of Manhattan, just three weeks earlier. The move took place on the day after my father's death. While my dad was going through chemotherapy in Palm Beach, Chris and I were in Los Angeles preparing to come to New York City for the delivery. We were making it a point to be in New York for Rowan's birth because we wanted her to have a New York City birth certificate. Toward the end of my pregnancy, my doctor hadn't allowed me to travel to Florida to visit my father, for fear I might go into labor away from the necessary medical expertise. I agreed to stay in Los Angeles until our scheduled trip to the Big Apple and honestly believed my father would hold on until after my daughter's birth. I had told Dad during our last visit together that I was going to bring the baby to meet him as soon as we were out of the hospital. I surprised him with the news that her middle name was going to be Francis, which was his given name, and added that she couldn't wait to meet her "Pop-Pop." I had called my paternal grandfather the same name and eagerly awaited this repeat of history. We were lying on his bed, and I remember a melancholy look in my dad's eyes as we talked. His breathing was labored, and he was having trouble speaking, but I could tell he was taking in what I was saying. I deeply hoped the prospect of meeting his granddaughter would give him strength and a will to survive, but it was not meant to be.

On the day of our departure from Los Angeles, my father gave up his fight against prostate cancer. I was at the dog park, trying to tire out Darla before our long flight east, when my cell phone rang. It was Diana, my stepsister, instructing me to tell my father whatever I wanted or needed to, because the end was near. Trying to sound calm, I told him I had always felt lucky he was my father and that I didn't want him to be scared. He couldn't respond, but my younger sister, Cristiana, said he wiggled his toes. Three hours later, with the entire family around him (except me), my dad left this earth. With very little time to process the information, I got on the red-eye with my husband, dog, and huge belly and cried all the way to New York.

We arrived in Manhattan early the next morning and had only a few hours to sleep before our co-ed baby shower was to occur in our new apartment. The place was the perfect site for a party because the only furniture we had was a bed, an armchair, a table, and Chris's old dresser from childhood. The party was lovingly given by a group of our friends. When they asked if I wanted to cancel the event because of my loss, I said my dad would've wanted it to go on. We made it a celebration of life, and in my mind, I pretended my father was simply still in Palm Beach. The shower was bittersweet but quite beautiful, and I'm sure Dad would've made a great toast. Rowan arrived a day before my dad's birthday, and I know he would have considered her a wonderful gift.

Though I couldn't wait to get out of the hospital, it was a sad homecoming for these first-time parents and their baby. History had already been infused into our new home; returning to its rather sterile surroundings and high ceilings, I was quickly reminded of that fateful day three weeks earlier.

As I hobbled to our bed, Rowan began crying. Her diaper needed changing, and because she was continuing to eliminate meconium, it looked like it was filled with licorice. I was still experiencing severe carpal tunnel syndrome, and my hands were unbelievably numb. They looked like they belonged to an old prizefighter, and since I had hardly any feeling in them, I couldn't manipulate

Rowan's harness or diaper effectively. Chris had to come to the rescue, and I labored back to bed, frustrated and in pain. As Chris adeptly navigated the industrial-strength Velcro attachments of the baby's contraption and wrestled with her harness, she screamed. Her screams echoed through the whole apartment. Though spacious, the place started to feel very small. I stayed on the bed and stared at an empty wall in front of me.

At first I thought what I was feeling was just exhaustion, but with it came an overriding sense of panic that I had never felt before. Rowan kept crying, and I began to dread the moment when Chris would bring her back to me. I started to experience a sick sensation in my stomach; it was as if a vise were tightening around my chest. Instead of the nervous anxiety that often accompanies panic, a feeling of devastation overcame me. I hardly moved. Sitting on my bed, I let out a deep, slow, guttural wail. I wasn't simply emotional or weepy, like I had been told I might be. This was something quite different. In the past, if I got depressed or if I felt sad or down, I knew I could counteract it with exercise, a good night's sleep, or a nice dinner with a friend. If PMS made me introspective or melancholy, or if the pressures of life made me gloomy, I knew these feelings wouldn't last forever. But this was sadness of a shockingly different magnitude. It felt as if it would never go away.

In general, I have always loved babies, and Rowan was not only amazing and alert but also quite beautiful. Her features were perfectly formed, and she looked like an angel. But I felt no appreciation for the little miracle. Although I didn't dislike her, I wasn't sure I wanted her living with us. In addition, I could hardly stand on my own two feet because of the sheer mass and weight of my body. If I had been in the mood to joke, I probably would have made a comparison between me and a sumo wrestler, but I had lost my sense of humor. I had become bruised and sore because my skin had expanded and been stretched so tightly it ached. My ankles and wrists looked like they had tight rubber bands around them. The indented skin had become dry and cracked. Besides the fact that I was physically incapable of performing many of the basic mothering duties, I also didn't feel like I wanted to get too close to Rowan. I wasn't afraid she was too fragile; I just felt no desire to pick her up. Every time I have ever been near a baby, any baby, I have always wanted to hold the child. It shocked me that I didn't want to hold my own daughter. I wished I had *I Dream of Jeannie* powers so I could blink myself into a warm, loving embrace with Rowan. Instead I was more like the distant and unsympathetic Endora from *Bewitched*.

I felt guilty for not being the one tending to my daughter, so I forced myself off the bed and waddled over to the old dresser that was substituting for a changing table. We hadn't yet gotten the nursery in place. I stared down at the tiny infant whose cheeks were dark red and whose eyes were like the Grand Canyon, and I began to feel faint. The plastic from the diapers they had given us at the hospital had a powdery odor, and the minute I smelled it, my knees got weak and I almost threw up. One whiff and I might as well have been back on the operating table. Again I thought it was due to sleep deprivation, but I couldn't stand there one more minute smelling that plastic. I moved away and stood in silence.

I watched as Chris finished the diapering, and felt like a beached whale. I was failing at things that, according to popular belief, were supposed to be the most natural in a woman's life. I had never been uncomfortable around babies, and they always responded positively to me. In fact, it sometimes surprised people when their babies opened their arms to me so quickly. Everybody always said that I would make a great mom one day.

I tried to rationalize that I was physically impaired and should give myself a break, but I didn't have any desire to power through and care for this baby. I got hit with a wave of self-defeat and self-loathing and had an urge to smash my head against the wall repeatedly. Chris told me to get off my feet and back into bed. Once there, my crying recommenced, and I started strongly believing that I couldn't be a mother. I was already proving to be incompetent, and we hadn't been home a day! What had I done? Why didn't I want to be near my baby?

I had little time to contemplate such thoughts, because it was time for Rowan to eat again (or snack, I should say). Without the help of a nurse or a lactation specialist, I was in trouble once more. I accepted Chris's help as he guided the baby's mouth onto my nipple; this time I didn't become annoyed or impatient with him or myself. I sat there almost catatonically, staring out into space. Rowan's nursing made me feel drugged and temporarily comforted me. But the moment she was finished and taken from me, I started to sob once more. I sat up with my huge legs stretched out in front of me and, slowly rocking back and forth with my face up toward the ceiling, my arms limp at my sides, I sobbed. I couldn't stop. What was I going to do? Was I ever going to stop feeling like this? Misery enveloped me.

I really needed to rest, but we seemed to be in an unrelenting routine of sporadic sleep, baby care, and lots of tears. The baby would wake up every hour and a half, and I would struggle to get her latched on. By the time she was on and had eaten a meal (if she stayed awake long enough to finish one), it was time to start all over again. Just as I would begin to fall into an exhausted sleep, Rowan's little bark, like Chinese water torture, would wake me up. This schedule continued incessantly and, thinking that it would be like this forever, I began to feel delirious. I was practically inconsolable. I couldn't stand any of it.

Chris and I were alone, and there was a great deal of silence in between my bouts of crying. Often he would break the silence by asking me to please tell him what was wrong. My response would be to shake my head and say I didn't know. There are many times where Chris and I are together and are not talking. It is a comforting thing that our silences have never been uneasy. This silence was very different. It was heavy and did not stem from a place of ease.

I had never felt emotion like this, and I strongly believed that even if I could articulate what I was experiencing, nobody would understand, not even my husband. And if he did understand, he certainly wouldn't be able to help. Chris kept doing all he could to keep the baby contented while continuing to try to talk to me. I knew he must be tired, too, but we couldn't seem to get on a schedule that allowed one of us to sleep while the other tended to the infant. Plus, I was afraid to let Chris sleep, because I was scared to be alone. Even though we were in the same apartment, if he was sleeping and I was awake, I thought I might try to escape or wouldn't be able to stop myself from swallowing a bottle of pills. I even thought that I'd welcome being kidnapped. These were strange, irrational fears that still felt real to me. I couldn't hand the baby completely over to Chris, either, because I wasn't yet producing enough milk to pump so he could feed her. I was hesitant to pump, anyway, because in the lactation class, we were warned about the horrors of "nipple confusion": One taste of a rubber nipple, and we might lose our babies to the bottle forever. So, like a zombie, at each feeding I would hold her tiny body at the appropriate angle and stare out the window.

Around this time, Chris took a photo of me. I'm holding the baby and looking straight at the camera. My hair looks like it hasn't been washed, and I'm slumped heavily in a chair with the baby wedged into the crook of my left arm. She looks sleepy and my smile seems forced. My eyes have a distant look, even though my gaze is directed right at the lens. To this day it makes my mother-in-law cry. She told me recently that she calls it "Vacant Eyes," and it breaks her heart to think of how lost I seemed.

After only a couple of days of being home, my crying had increased and no longer occurred only in between feedings but during them as well. At times I even had trouble holding Rowan because of my choking sobs. Why was I crying more than my baby? Here I was, finally the mother of a beautiful baby girl I had worked so hard to have, and I felt like my life was over. Where was the bliss? Where was the happiness that I had expected to feel by becoming a mother? She was my baby; the baby I had wanted for so long. Why didn't I feel remotely comforted by having or holding her? I had always felt that a baby was the one major thing missing from my life, that a child would complete the picture and bring everything into focus. Once I was a mother, the different parts of my world would all converge, and I would experience life as I'd envisioned it and in turn would know what I was meant to be. But having a baby clouded my vision and threatened whatever peace had already existed. Instead of wanting to move forward, all I wanted was for life to return to the way it was before I had Rowan.

I longed for the freedom to pick up and go to the movies or on a hike or a trip out of the country. Chris and I used to go on spontaneous trips and mini-vacations. Sometimes I would take a job in a city that we hadn't been to, and we'd extend the trip and explore. We could sleep when we wanted to and make our own schedule, depending on how we felt. Because our work is versatile, we could find ourselves stateside one day and needing a passport the next. Even if we were home, we managed to be creative and stayed busy.

I love schedules but prefer to be the person making them. It occurred to me that my life was no longer my own and that I was a prisoner to a small, squeaking creature. I did not like it one bit. I felt stuck. I did not want the responsibility this situation demanded. I started feeling like I had made a terrible mistake in having this child. I would look at how little and vulnerable she was and didn't feel at all capable of tending to her needs. Her helplessness terrified me. Rather than wanting to care for her, I wanted to forget her and run away.

Sometimes when I went to the bathroom and tried not to gag at the blood and "stuff" that continuously came pouring out of my body, I wondered how the human race survived. Why would anyone do this more than once? I had thought that it would all get better once we got home, but it was unbelievably worse. I felt no connection to my daughter and wanted to die because of it. She grew inside my body, for God's sake, and I didn't even feel related to her. I had always thought I would immediately feel closer to my child than I did to anybody else in my life. I'd thought we would be undeniably bonded from the moment I laid eyes on her. What was wrong with me? What a horrible mother I was! Her cry didn't annoy me or grate on my nerves, but it also didn't register with me, either. I felt numb to it. I practically had to strain to hear her voice, which seemed so far away, even though she was in the adjoining room and the door was open. I could almost justify not hearing it.

My profound detachment made me suffer unbearably, and I believed I had nowhere to turn. I remember looking out of the bedroom window and envisioning myself jumping. I concluded that it wouldn't be too effective, because we weren't high enough. This upset me even more. The frightening part was that my thoughts were extremely rational. They made clear sense to me. It felt like an appealing option to erase myself from this life. What would stop me from acting on any of these thoughts? I needed and wanted a way out. My mind was full of visions of escape, and these constantly overshadowed thoughts about my miraculous baby girl.

During what was becoming one of the darkest points in my life, I sat holding my newborn and could not avoid the image of her flying through the air and hitting the wall in front of me. I had no desire to hurt my baby and didn't see myself as the one throwing her, thank God, but the wall morphed into a video game, and in it her little body smacked the surface and slid down onto the floor. I was horrified, and although I knew deep in my soul that I would not harm her, the image all but destroyed me.

I was desperate to have a natural and healthy connection with my daughter, but it was feeling so forced. It was as if I were trapped behind a thick glass wall. I had never felt apathy in my life, and when I had least expected it, it crept in and took over. I couldn't shake the feeling of doom and gloom that pervaded each moment. I was afraid of myself and felt threatened by the dangerous thoughts running so calmly through my head. They all felt too real. When would I wake up from this bad dream?

I started calling friends and family and crying to them on the phone. I told my friend Linda in California that I didn't want a baby anymore. She joked that if worse came to worst, she would raise the baby with Chris. She said she knew I'd be fine, but she thought it would help me to talk to a girlfriend of hers who had similar thoughts when she had her child. I had met the person she was referring to but didn't know her very well. It seemed pathetic to call a basic stranger to talk about my feelings toward my newborn, so I never made that call.

I then called my stepsister Diana and asked her to promise me it would get better. She reassured me that it would, but begged me to get a baby nurse for a few days so I could sleep. The people in my life were trying to help, but I was in over my head. I was afraid to be left alone with my child not because I thought I'd do anything to her but because the thought of being the only person to care for her terrified me. I was equally afraid to be left alone with my emotions. I thought that maybe if I shone a spotlight on myself, I wouldn't do anything stupid or fall further into the dark pit I was in. Everyone said it would pass and that it would all turn out okay. I kept hearing how normal these feelings were and how I would get over them. I knew, however, that I was the only person who would never get over them. This dark cloud would never lift. I called my girlfriend Sherie and cried. She, too, is an actress, and we have worked together on various projects. I knew she would understand. When I told her I wanted my old life back, she said, "This baby was meant to come into your life. Look at all you and Chris went through to have her! You are supposed to be her home." For a brief moment this type of thinking provided a bit of relief, but it was fleeting. Yeah, look at all we went through! Then why aren't I happy?

The routine of feeding and crying was endless, and it seemed there was no relief in sight. After being on this treadmill for about five days, Chris went out to a store to buy a changing table. We thought that if the baby's room was more set up, it would lift my mood and help me get into the whole baby experience. He came back sooner than expected and without the table. He walked into the bedroom and sat down on the bed in silence. He looked up at me, his eyes filled with tears, and broke down. I was speechless but begged him with my own eyes to tell me what was wrong. Through tears that I had only ever seen at happy times, he began saying, "There were women in the store who were happy, Brooke! They were smiling and happy to have their babies! What's wrong with you? Why aren't you happy? You don't look at Rowan or sing to her or talk to her. Why? What's happening?"

I could hardly breathe; I felt as if I had been punched in the gut. Here was the most sensitive and consistently strong man I had ever known being beaten down by the woman he loved. I had created this situation and had no answer to give him. I had never seen him this helpless before. It scared me, because he was my safety net, and now he was falling apart at my doing. All I could say was, "I don't know. I am sorry. I am so sorry." I felt more powerless at that moment than I have ever felt in my life: I was paralyzed. I sensed a weight on top of me, pressing down. What was wrong with me? When would this feeling stop? The sadness was smothering me.

I plummeted deeper into despair at the thought that our little girl could feel my lack of warmth. From the first moment I laid eyes on her, she appeared to be a wise little soul. Her gaze was that of a much older person rather than of someone who had just entered the world. Her eyes appeared to have a knowing and judgmental look. I remember feeling that when she looked at me, she knew everything about me. At this particular period in our lives together, she didn't show any understanding of my despair, but because I have always believed in the intelligence and sensitivity of infants, I was further punished by a strong belief that she knew how I was feeling. I was in my own hell and was jealous of all the women in that store and of everyone else's ability to enjoy their children. I remained incapable of responding to Chris or Rowan. I just sat there sobbing. Chris left the room and tried to recover from his own torture. Seeing him go, I hung my head, and the hot, thick tears dropped out of my eyes and hit the bedspread.

This was far worse than any PMS that I had ever experienced, and it was not showing any signs of dissipating. My PMS moodiness usually manifested itself by my being quiet or slightly edgy and needing to be alone for a day or so. In contrast, this felt like my life was over and I would never be happy again. I felt like a failure, and had tremendous guilt about not feeling close to my baby, but there was no way to explain the situation to anybody.

I would listen as Chris animatedly talked on the phone. I'd hear snippets of conversations in which he would talk about how amazing the baby was. Then there would be a pause, and he'd say, "Brooke's doing okay; she's just struggling a bit because of the C-section and the swelling in her hands." When he concluded that I'd be fine, I could tell he was hoping this would happen.

He spoke to my mom and to his own parents and eventually agreed that maybe they should come and help us out. As a sort of watchful-eye tag team, they began alternating caring for the baby and observing me. Everyone seemed to think I just needed rest and that this would soon come to pass. They took turns staying in the TV/library/den/playroom on an air mattress. The doors to the area slide open directly into the living/dining room. Needless to say, the quarters were tight and far from comfortable. I was embarrassed by the clumsiness of it all but didn't have an ounce of energy to make it better. This went on for about ten days, and I have to admit that even under the best of conditions, living with parents or in-laws is not a recipe for relaxation. I will say, however, that I was so incapacitated mentally and physically, I didn't pay much attention to what was going on around me. The parents came and went, and I retreated to my bed. I remained stoic and uninvolved but hardly rested. Rowan was primarily brought to me to feed. I would sometimes get mini-lectures from my mom about how lucky I was to have been blessed with this incredible child and how I was going to be fine. On one particular day, while my mom was on duty, I dragged myself out of bed to sit at the dining room table with her. She looked at me with a mixture of concern and frustration.

"You wanted this baby so badly, and you always get everything you want, so try to be happy. You are so lucky, my love, and I know you will be feeling better very soon. It's only been a little while. Give yourself a break. You are always so impatient. She's so beautiful and so lovable."

I responded in a monotone. "She doesn't love me. I know it."

"Of course she does! You're her mother."

"That doesn't make any difference. I don't feel any connection to her." I felt so empty inside. Words couldn't do it justice.

"Now, Brookie, don't talk like that. Please!"

"I can't help it. I don't want to be here. I am so unhappy, and it will never get better. I hate myself. I am so sad, I'm just so sad. This is horrible. I just want to die."

My mom became visibly scared. Her face paled, her mouth got dry, and the circles under her eyes seemed to get darker. It's not often that I've seen her like that, and I was struck by her expression. Out of desperation, she quietly said, "Remember how devastated you felt when David killed himself? You don't want to do the same to those who love you."

All I could do was stare back at her.

David Strickland had been like a brother to me. For three seasons and almost four years, we had worked together on *Suddenly Susan*. We met before the show started and instantly became the best of friends. I had never become this close to someone this fast, and it was like a sigh of relief to know we'd be friends for life. We were rarely apart and loved each other dearly. Ever since his suicide, in 1999, not a day goes by when I don't think of him. My life was irreparably changed the day he died, and I miss him terribly. Obviously my mother's plea did not help my mood except possibly to give me a better understanding of how desperate my poor friend may have been feeling toward the end. I began thinking that maybe I should just go join David and my father and leave everyone else here on earth.

"But Mom, it has gotten so bad that this morning I made Chris cry."

My mother misunderstood me. "I made him cry?"

"No, Mom! *I* made him cry, this is not about you! *I* made him cry." I started to scream at her. "GET OUT! GET OUT NOW, OR I'LL JUMP OUT OF THE FUCKING WINDOW!"

Now it was my mother's turn to stare. My tolerance had worn thin, and a mother is an easy target. She sat in stunned silence. Perhaps she thought that if she was still enough, this nightmare would pass. She didn't leave, and I was relieved by her decision not to. I felt bad for her, but I was like a caged animal, ready to charge while cowering in the corner. I didn't know where to turn.

Everyone believed that activity in the household might at least keep me distracted, so a steady stream of close friends began visiting in shifts. My friend Brenda flew in for a night and ended up sleeping on a chaise with our dog, Darla. Under normal circumstances, I never would have let someone sleep on a chaise; I would have given up my own bed first. But I didn't think to care about this. Who was I?

Another friend, Jaymeson, had had her second child only three weeks before I had Rowan. I had assisted with the birth. Such a short time after that amazingly beautiful and encouraging experience, she packed one baby on her chest and the other on her back and took the subway to my apartment from the opposite end of town. I was sitting somberly in my bed when she arrived. She cried a bit when she saw me and immediately asked if I had eaten. I couldn't remember if I had or not, and she ran to get one of our favorite sandwiches. Upon her return, she said she'd visit often and that I had to try to get some consecutive hours of sleep. She asked if my doctor had mentioned anything about taking medication and that I might want to look into it. I hadn't even told my doctor what I was feeling. It was just too shameful. I reminded Jaymeson that I wasn't one to take drugs and would rather delay or avoid such drastic measures. Following our visit, she packed up her happy team and returned to her nanny-free home like Superwoman. She had such ease with her kids and seemed to be so connected to them. She did say it wasn't always easy but that in the big picture, it was such a joyful experience. My own picture was getting uglier and uglier, and each time someone left, I felt my eyesight narrow. You know how, just before fainting, your peripheral vision starts to darken and the sound in the room gets muffled? I felt that way every time a visitor left my apartment. I began to fear time without distraction.

My girlfriend Lyda, who had been in the room for Rowan's birth, came over and brought Rowan a beautiful letter she had written to welcome her into the world. I wished I had written the letter but would once again have to live vicariously through other loving eyes. Lyda again commented on Rowan's often funny expressions and on how judgmental and unimpressed she still seemed. I explained that she probably knew her mother was horrible and it made her hate me. Lyda detected my seriousness and said I should get some temporary help with the baby so I could get back on track. A friend of hers had had a hard time as well and had gotten a nanny for a short period of time so she could catch up on her rest enough to gain an altered perspective. A nanny was not going to solve my detachment as a mother, but I took the phone number and said I'd make the call.

Lyda and I have known each other basically since we were in our mothers' wombs. Since we'd been friends for so long, she knew me well: She could tell I was not in good shape. She had recently lost her mother to cancer and gently reminded me that on top of everything else, I had never had a chance to process my father's death. That alone was a tremendous amount to deal with under any circumstance. There was validity to what she said, but it didn't help shake my mood.

As many friends called or came with encouragement and empathy, nothing seemed to help. Everyone continued to marvel at Rowan's beauty and alertness. They would say, "But come on, aren't you in love?" Trying to be honest, I'd reply, "Not yet," but the truth was I felt nothing. Had they all immediately felt such love for their babies? My child was a source of joy to everyone who came into contact with her, except me. I couldn't believe I was missing out on all of the happiness they described and which I had so anticipated. I had been waiting to be overwhelmed by the deepest love fathomable, and all I felt was distance and dread. Nothing was as I had pictured it.

I had enjoyed a wonderful pregnancy and had honestly never felt better in my life. I never had morning sickness and felt energetic and strong. I had done yoga until the day Rowan was born and hadn't gained any more weight than the healthy, suggested amount.

I felt sexy and proud of how I looked. I reveled in the image of the female and the maternal and was engulfed by the peace these feelings created. I perpetuated this image by appearing on the cover of *Vogue* magazine pregnant and looking like I was enjoying true harmony with life. The best part was that it wasn't forced. I was genuinely healthy and happy and eagerly awaited the union with my child and the continued joy I knew it would bring. I'd talked to my stomach and felt bonded with the fetus. I have many pictures of my pregnancy that capture this feeling of contentment. Then, after almost nine months of bliss, everything went horribly awry. My present reality was the antithesis of everything I had expected, and I was desperate for the connection and pure joy I thought I would have experienced in motherhood. By this point, my marital relationship was in a holding pattern. I was so consumed by fear and by mental torture that I was oblivious to anything going on outside of my own head.

Being awake was incredibly painful emotionally, and as anyone who has ever had a baby knows, you don't spend too much time sleeping. Days and nights blended into one another, and I saw no light at the end of the dark tunnel. Meanwhile, various friends and relatives were giving Chris a lot of advice. He was stuck in the middle and had to decide how much information to convey to me. He didn't explain the extent of my despair to his parents; everyone thought I was just very tired and recovering from major surgery. He was scared about my emotional state, but he didn't want to embarrass me by telling anyone else. He also didn't want to worry anybody.

Both my mother-in-law and my mother suggested that I stop breast-feeding to give myself a break. In fact, the consensus seemed to be that I give up the baby on the breast and move past that added pressure. But what nobody understood was that the breast-feeding was my only real connection to the baby. If I were to eliminate that, I might have no hope of coming through this nightmare. I was hanging on to the breast-feeding as my lifeline. It was the only thing that made me unique in terms of caring for her, and it created an undeniable connection, even if only a physical one. Without it, she might be lost to me forever. If I continued, maybe I would eventually become less cut off from my own flesh and blood. I wanted to recede into the distance, but her mouth on my body kept forcing me to be present. I refused to quit.

When it was time to take myself and the baby for our first post natal visit, Rowan was as quiet as a mouse, while I was the one who broke down. It quickly turned into a lengthy mommy checkup. While the baby sat with Chris and a nurse, Dr. Rebarber guided me into an empty exam room so we could talk. I told him I was not doing well at all and explained through my sobs that I couldn't take care of this baby. I just didn't want to do it. I told him that I felt I had no relationship to her. Because I felt so ashamed, I probably sounded stronger than I felt. He said to trust him, that this feeling would pass and that many new mothers went through the baby blues. He explained that it had to do with the fact that out with the placenta went many of the hormones contributing to the sense of well-being I had felt during the pregnancy. Once the hormones equalized, I would start feeling better. He said the hormonal shifts that occur post natal are often a shock to women, but even his wife went through it, and it was very normal. He, too, suggested that I not breast-feed. I couldn't even explain my theory on why I needed to keep doing it. He was so warm and caring, and he had been right about everything before. I stopped crying long enough to admit that I felt I had made a mistake by having a baby. He looked at me seriously and said, "You know what, Brooke? I'm not God. I can only do my best, but if that baby was not meant to be here, she wouldn't be." He had sure seemed godlike to me when he so adeptly saved my daughter's life, as well as my own, so I decided to trust him, once again. Maybe it was hormonal, or maybe I was one of those emotional women who was making more out of it than necessary. Even though it appeared to be more serious than a hormonal imbalance, I would try mind over matter. I felt too ashamed to keep trying to convince him it was otherwise. The doctor said he would keep checking on me and that it might help if I talked to other mothers I knew and got their perspective. In addition to referring us to a pediatrician, he suggested we both come back in a week. Rowan would surely be fine, but to me a week sounded like an eternity. We left the office and I tried to feel encouraged.

As I reentered the apartment, the same feelings came flooding in like a bursting of Hoover Dam. My friend Sherie came over with a stack of information on post natal depression that she'd printed out from the Internet. She explained that everything I had said to her on the phone was repeated practically verbatim in this material. She also brought me two books on different women's accounts— one from the early 1990s and one that looked like a medical textbook—and begged me to page through them. I couldn't imagine that any of the material could possibly have anything to do with me. Plus, the last thing I wanted to do was read information about other people's lives or on how "common" my feelings were. I was certain that nobody else could possibly feel what I was feeling. She might as well have been giving me information on penile enlargement; it was that irrelevant to me. Post natal depression was a crazy person's affliction, and I associated it only with those people who harmed their kids by doing things like driving the car into a lake. I was certainly not in that category. I had no intention of ever harming my baby, although I also didn't seem to have any intention of becoming attached to her, either. I was a healthy-minded and capable woman who simply shouldn't have had a child. Post natal depression was plainly not something that affected someone like me. It hit only those people you read about in the news.

I must admit that although I'm always available to listen to other people's problems, I am not always quick to divulge when something is really bothering me. I will rant about daily issues but keep the deep stuff buried. Chris calls it "That Last 5 Percent." It takes a long time, if at all, for people to register with me that deeply, and it has kept many a friend at an uncomfortable distance. Often, after trying, people just give up. I have probably been perfecting this self-defense technique my whole life, and though it has served me well as a protective mechanism, I did not want it to rear its ugly head now. It did not feel like the appropriate time to stay so removed from other people. It felt dangerous to do so. I had to consciously reach out for help. If I didn't, maybe I'd retreat so far that I'd disappear. I made another round of phone calls and, sounding even more desperate than before, I asked my godmother, Lila, to pray for me and decided I'd ask another friend to come and visit.

The person I asked to visit was Rowan's godfather, John. He was there for me after my friend David died and after I had my miscarriage. Although no longer an agent, he had been mine for years and had seen me through many a low point in my personal and professional life. He was not only a close friend but someone who had always understood me and encouraged me in all areas of my life. He knew me well, and I wanted him to see me in my current state. Maybe he would shed some light on my situation, but more than anything, I needed his support.

He flew to New York and came straight to see us. He walked in, and, seeing his face, I immediately got choked up. I told him I didn't believe there was relief for me and that not only was my life being destroyed, I was hurting those around me. I was remarkably rational and calm as I told him that I couldn't be a mother and I didn't even really want to live if my life was going to continue like this. I felt possessed by some force. He said that since he had known me, he had never heard me utter such words. In a tone full of empathy and not an ounce of condescension, he suggested I get some sort of professional help. He said that I ought to think about hiring some baby care as well, until I felt more like myself. Hearing him reiterate that I was not, in fact, myself gave me a glimmer of hope. It indicated that what I was feeling was not who I was and that maybe I could be cured.

John held Rowan, and this time I lived vicariously through his reactions to her. He kept reveling in how perfect she was. He spoke to her with such tenderness; my heart felt as if it were shattering. He said he knew I loved her, and I explained that I hoped I did but that this strangely had nothing to do with loving her. I knew deep inside

I must love her. She was my daughter, after all, but it didn't seem to make any difference. I just didn't *feel* anything for her. In addition, I felt such hatred and sadness for myself. It was impossible to understand or grasp. I had never experienced such self-loathing before. I was comforted only by the fact that I knew deep down I didn't want anything bad to happen to my daughter. I would surely die if it did. Yet I still couldn't climb out of this abyss and fully respond to who she was. I reiterated to John that I didn't think I could be a mother, and he repeated that not only did he know I was capable of anything I put my mind and heart to, but I actually had no choice. The words "no choice" terrified me. I told John the problem was that I couldn't reach my heart or my mind. I couldn't and I didn't want to. He made me promise to speak to the doctor again, gave me a long hug, and swore I'd be okay. When he departed, I wanted to run out the door with him.

Again Diana called to check up on me. She urged me to please get a baby nurse. Her husband said to think of it as an investment in my sanity and in my marriage. We never imagined it would be so hard to take care of a 7½-pound baby. We also never anticipated that I would be so incapacitated. Chris said he thought it might be a good idea to get some help, especially while he was away. He would have to return to Los Angeles for work and was feeling extremely anxious about leaving me alone. He couldn't understand why I still wasn't happy but thought maybe a baby nurse might offer at least a modicum of relief.

Even though I wasn't able to communicate well with him, I still needed him near me. I was afraid to have him leave, and I didn't want to be completely alone with my baby. I worried I'd be unable to respond to her needs. I had been retreating more and more each day, and my husband was feeling helpless. For over two weeks, I had done hardly anything except robotically shuffle around, unable to even really speak. I couldn't believe a baby nurse would help a marriage, but if things continued like this, then our relationship would be damaged. For the time being, the baby seemed unscathed, but Chris and I would surely benefit from some assistance.

Since my checkup, Dr. Rebarber had been phoning me daily to see how I was doing. During one of his calls, he told me that while almost all women experienced some form of the baby blues, many also suffered from the more acute post natal depression. He had been thinking about the look on my face and about what I'd said to him regarding my mood, and because it sounded so severe and so out of character, he suggested I might want to see a therapist and even try some medication. Since John's visit, I had been considering a therapist but hadn't followed through. As far as medication was concerned, it was out of the question, because I was still breast-feeding and had no intention of stopping. Dr. Rebarber explained that there was medicine I could take that wouldn't get into my milk or affect the baby. I said I had to think about it but did not like the idea of taking medicine. None of the women I knew of had needed medication after giving birth, and I felt I shouldn't, either. In my entire life, I had never needed drugs to help with my moods and didn't want to start now. It was yet another sign of my weakness and failure as a mother. I hung up the phone feeling even more hopeless, like I was being tortured. This was indeed a losing battle.

I told my husband about Dr. Rebarber's suggestions, and he exhaled with relief. Maybe more help did exist. Chris knew I was upset at the prospect of taking drugs, so he gently explained that many people took medication for a myriad of reasons and that there was nothing wrong with it. It wouldn't have to be forever, and if it made me feel better, it was worth a try. In under three weeks, I had managed to terrify everyone who cared for me, and now my husband wanted me to become a pill popper! Once again, *One Flew Over the Cuckoo's Nest* came to mind, and I saw myself in pajamas, shuffling up to the nurse's window to get my little cup of pills. Why not start drinking Scotch at three in the afternoon and take up cigarettes, too? I couldn't face the thought of being dependent on medication to feel better, especially when all my dreams had supposedly just come true by having a baby.

CHAPTER 4

SEE MOMMY RUN

THE IDEA OF TAKING MEDICINE to deal with a psychological problem scared me. I had always believed I could solve my own problems in a natural and healthy way and was ashamed by the thought that I might need drugs. I came from a family of alcoholics and feared addiction myself. But the truth was that everyone was thriving in my household except me. Rowan was doing incredibly well. She was eating like a truck driver and pooping like a champ. What came out of her body was the correct color for her age, and she had no signs of diaper rash. She was smiling a great deal, and I swear it was not just gas! Chris had adapted beautifully to his new role as a father. He bathed and changed the baby as if he had been doing it his entire life. He already had nicknames for her, like "Bugaboo Jones" and "Muggins McGee," and I would hear him sing her songs incorporating these names. I'd listen and ache to be able to interact with the baby in such a carefree way. He was reveling in his role as caretaker, and I was continuing to miss out.

I finally called my doctor and said I would try medication but only if he promised I wouldn't get addicted and that I wouldn't have to be on it forever. He said he could start me off with a low dose of Paxil, an antidepressant, and that it was nonaddictive, safe for breast-feeding, and I would take it only for a few months. This sounded fair, but I was afraid that the world would know I was on medication and think I was weak or crazy. I decided that the only people who needed to know about it were me, Chris, and the doctor. I got the prescription but had no faith it would even work. I was feeling so bad that I found it hard to believe a tiny pink pill could lift the black cloud following me around like Pigpen from *Peanuts*. I believed that this really wasn't a medical issue and entertained the thought that the doctors were probably going to give me a placebo anyway. I was obviously beginning to get paranoid. I begrudgingly took the first dose and waited to feel instantly and miraculously better. I was told the drug might take as long as two weeks to start working and not to be impatient. Here I was, feeling worse than I had ever felt in my life, and I was supposed to be patient! Patience has never been one of my strong points, and I got even more frustrated. The baby was already over two weeks old, and I was the only one who wasn't making any progress.

I considered walking out of the front door and never coming back. I could just calmly leave and enjoy my freedom for a while before being discovered wandering upstate. I could probably get in three good days before even being recognized. In reality, I couldn't leave, but I believed that if I did, Rowan would be fine without me. In fact, she might be better off. This idea drew me in, and I spent time fantasizing about disappearing forever. The problem was that after I enjoyed the relief I found in such a daydream, reality invariably slapped me in the face. I discovered that I could escape for short times in the shower. I would hide in there the minute Rowan was done with her midmorning feeding. I couldn't take naps, since she was up and eating every ninety minutes, so a shower was my only respite. The showers got longer, and I would often sit on the floor under the flow of scalding water and cry. Sometimes I'd sneak in another shower during the afternoon. Nobody commented on it, but they probably thought that my attention to hygiene was a good sign as far as depression was concerned.

The day before the in-laws left, we all went to see a matinee of the play 9. The doctor said it was okay to take the baby out because my breast milk was giving her the antibodies and protection she needed. Getting dressed up and being out were frightening but necessary. I did not have my friends to help this time and had even less energy to care about how I looked, but I managed to find an all-black outfit that fit, and I put my hair in a ponytail. Because nobody other than the stage manager knew we were going to the theater, I wasn't concerned about photographers. I did worry that I might have a panic attack in the theater or maybe start crying and want to run out. In any case, I knew that the outing would be an important test. I was curious to see how it would feel to be in the outside world after being so secluded. Chris encouraged the excursion to get me out of the house and to prove that I could do things like this even though I'd had a baby. I couldn't, however, breast-feed during the play. Chris suggested I try the breast pump just this once. Although exhausted, I didn't resist at all. I needed to feel that everything in my world was still normal. In my mind, having the baby had made my life hopeless and meant that nothing would ever be the way it used to be.

I managed to get 4 ounces into a bottle; at this point, nipple confusion was the least of my worries. Then we put the baby in the Baby-Björn, and headed to the theater. Rowan still had to wear her harness, but she fit into the Björn without a problem. A number of people on this production team had worked on *Cabaret* and were good friends of mine. And because I knew the company manager extremely well, we were able to leave Rowan in the office with her during the play. This woman had looked after me during the run of *Cabaret*, and I had spent a great deal of time alone with her before and after September 11. She had even helped me with the IVF shots. I trusted her. I gave her instructions about feeding and changing Rowan and said that if the baby got fussy, an usher should come and find me. As I exited the small room without my daughter, I felt like I was slinking away from responsibility. It should have made me nervous to leave a newborn, but I trusted these people. They had known about my struggles to have a baby and had been concerned all along. My experience with Broadway people is that they legitimately care for one another and come to the rescue when necessary. Shamefully, I also felt relief to leave the baby with them. As I walked down the stairs, I had an urge to take off running; instead, I went quietly into the theater. I did feel guilty for wanting to be without my baby but was equally thrilled by the prospect of not hearing her voice for a while.

As Chris, his parents, and I went to our seats, I searched other people's faces. I wondered if they could tell what I was feeling or if any other mothers in the theater were in the same state as me. The play began, and watching it, I craved being onstage again. I wanted to leave my world and jump back into the more selfishly carefree and single-minded existence of life in the theater. There was a freedom in performing, and I felt I would never be able to experience it again. I became aware that, as a mother, your priorities get switched, and I felt surprisingly resentful. In my mind, being a mother meant not being able to be onstage. It was an irrational thought, but according to my current state of mind, having a baby commanded an all-or-nothing approach; I didn't believe in the possibility of balance. I wasn't sure I was ready for such an ultimatum. I didn't realize that I was the one who had made it.

At intermission we went back up to the office, and Rowan was sound asleep. She had drunk her bottle and been happily passed around from actor to actor. Chita Rivera couldn't stop talking about how beautiful she was, and Antonio Banderas gave her a kiss. I joked that I was the one who had given birth to her and deserved a kiss myself. I didn't get so lucky! Being out of the apartment offered a bit of a relief, due to the change of scenery, but my heart remained heavy and I felt like a fraud. People kept popping their heads into the office to say hi. My friends were thrilled to meet Rowan.

"Aren't you just thrilled to be a mother?"

"You must be so in love!"

"She is amazing!"

"What a blessing!"

"Congratulations!"

"Oh my God, she's beautiful."

All I could do was smile and say, "It's crazy."

Some of the girls in the cast who didn't have kids looked longingly at my "perfect" family. What they didn't know was that I would have stepped into their dance shoes in a New York minute. I said little except to mention that I was very tired. We saw Act II, and I left the theater feeling out of sorts. I wasn't sure who I was. I had been clinging to this notion that when a baby entered my life, everything would fall into place, and a rhythm would be established. Together my child and I would epitomize the image I had internalized from watching all those happy families on TV in my youth, with a dose of Norman Rockwell thrown in for good measure. In my mind, this was the perfect, blissful picture of motherhood I assumed I would experience when I had a baby.

We spent the rest of the afternoon at the hotel room of some friends who were visiting from Los Angeles—Steven Weber, a fellow actor, his wife, Juliette, and their two beautiful children. Although obviously harried, Steven and Juliette were madly in love with their offspring. Other friends of theirs, along with their three kids, joined us at the hotel. We all hung out in the room overlooking Central Park. Lots of food was brought in, and after I positioned myself on the bed in silence, I didn't move for hours. I fed Rowan and munched on Teddy Grahams while kids ran in and out of the room. The dads took a walk down to the bar for a drink, and the women stayed to tend to the kiddie chaos. These mothers all seemed so comfortable in their roles and so attuned to the needs of their kids. One of the children was an infant not much older than mine. I stared at the way this baby and her mother interacted and at the ease with which all the moms cared for their little ones. There was a lot of laughter and cuddling. I wanted to cry even more. These other moms didn't appear to want to be anywhere else and seemed at peace. Motherhood agreed with all of them. Rowan fell asleep and I just watched. The guys returned and brought with them another friend of mine whom they'd run into at the bar; she also happened to be staying at the hotel. She asked if she could hold Rowan. No argument here! My friend has red hair, and when I saw Rowan in her arms, I fantasized that she was the mother and I was just visiting.

What in the hell was wrong with me? Why wasn't I happy? I was hanging on to something and didn't know what it was. Why didn't I crave having Rowan in my arms? I felt incredibly guilty for wanting my old life back and also felt desperate to be a happy, loving, and present mother. It all felt wrong and utterly hopeless. Maybe the fact that I'd had such a hard time getting pregnant was nature's way of telling me I shouldn't have had kids. Guilt reared its ugly head, and I believed my current state was my punishment for trying to play God and for letting science interfere with what was so obviously not supposed to happen.

Chris had hoped that by being with other mothers, I would get encouraged, but instead I felt alienated. Juliette said I was doing very well. She was impressed that I had decided to forge ahead and continue breast-feeding, especially because so many of our friends had had such a hard time with it. I had dreamed of breast-feeding my whole life. Though I didn't realize it, I was guarding as sacred an idealized version of mother and child. I had even done a movie called *The Blue Lagoon* in which, after my character has a baby, the infant intuitively finds his way to my breast and starts to suck while I look on, smiling. I was only fifteen at the time and have had that image stuck in my mind for years. (Much to my chagrin, many a fourteen-year-old and dirty old man did as well.) Plus, I knew that if I didn't give myself every opportunity to succeed at breast-feeding, I'd feel like I had missed out and would regret it forever. I told Juliette I couldn't handle any more failure, and because it was the one thing I seemed to have a modicum of success with and "so far, so good," I was committed to continuing. I was lucky that Rowan was latching on and that I had no nipple problems. I couldn't believe I was actually discussing nipple issues!

Was I so adamant about Rowan getting mother's milk because I was being driven by my type A personality, or was I subconsciously more connected to her than I realized? Whatever the reason, it was a bona fide sign that I cared about her and wanted her to be nourished in the best way possible. It seemed to be one of the only maternal instincts that I had, and I clung to it.

Sometimes I would multitask or get on the phone while Rowan was nursing, and she would get mad and pull away. If I was preoccupied while feeding her, she became disquieted. It became clear to me, and to Chris, that even though it was the one thing that seemed to be going well, I was not allowing myself to relax into it and feel the joy that could result from such closeness. I made a deal with my husband that every time the baby was latched on, I would concentrate only on feeding her. I would sit alone with her and be calm and focused. I would not make calls or let my thoughts distract me. I quickly learned it was easier when I was more focused. I didn't completely enjoy it until much later, but Rowan kept me to my promise. I began feeling further justified for not giving it up because I noticed that while Rowan was on the teat, we were both noticeably more relaxed. My mother-in-law, my mother, my doctor, and even some other mothers who chose not to breast-feed finally stopped telling me to quit, and it became one less thing I had to fight for. Was the medicine helping, or was I just figuring things out?

Our families had all left New York, and Chris and I were alone again with the baby, but not for long. The time had come for him to go to Los Angeles for work. He was to be gone a whole week, and the thought of him leaving made me increasingly nervous. Later Chris would admit that he, too, was afraid to leave me alone, but he thought that if I managed well, it would give me some much needed confidence. I'd have access to friends and family, but for the majority of the time, it would be just me and the baby. This fact also unnerved me tremendously. Long ago Chris and I had worked out the logistics of being bicoastal. We had become acclimated to spending days apart, and our separations never lasted long. Though Chris was now used to flying back and forth between Los Angeles and New York, a baby had never been a part of the equation. I wasn't as upset that he was leaving as I was afraid to be isolated with my infant. I was also jealous that he was going and I was not. I wanted to go back to work, too. Work symbolized the escape I was seeking. It had always been my refuge; while concentrating on the job at hand, I could easily block out any of the bad stuff that may have been going on in my life. Currently I had nothing to take my mind off of my fears.

Physically I was more mobile, and a lot of the swelling in my body had gone down, but in no way was I back to normal. I hadn't been aware that it would affect me so, but watching Chris go back to work really shook me up. I kept making sweeping generalizations, like "I'll never be able to work again." I couldn't stop believing that this would be my only life from this day forward. Chris left one morning on an early flight, and I cried as he stepped into the elevator. I could tell that the fatigue and stress had gotten to him. He was pale and quiet and didn't seem half as inclined to be funny or make any of the jokes I had come to rely on in times of stress. I wanted to do or say something to make him, and me, feel better, but no matter what thought came to mind, it was negative:

"My life is over."

"I'll never feel connected to my daughter."

"I shouldn't have had a baby."

"I am a horrible mother."

"I made a terrible mistake."

"I can't do this."

"I'm so alone in how I feel."

"I am the only person in the world who won't ever be happy or in love with her child."

"I hate myself and I hate life."

"My daughter will never love me."

The voices in my head kept screaming, and I felt so sad.

Chris was a father, and he was able to return to his job almost immediately. No one encouraged my going back to work and the assumption was that I wouldn't even have the desire to do so. I, too, had believed that after having a child, I would choose staring at my baby over any job and that being a mom would usurp all else. I expected motherhood to be more of a relief from the pressures of my profession. I thought I would feel liberated, as if having a baby would give me permission to not work so hard.

Many actresses and businesswomen I knew had told me that the minute they had their kids, they no longer had the same ambitions, and that represented such a gift for them. One actress friend said, "Trust me, once you have your baby, you are not going to care one bit about this crazy business we are in. You won't even want to work!" I was so surprised that this was not what was happening. I felt like a horrible person. Once again my expectations were not coming to fruition. People would comment on how relieved I must be not to go back to work and to just be a mom for a while: "What a luxury it must be for you not to think about anything other than that baby!" Most people who know me (and even those who don't) believe that because I have worked since I was a little girl, I must have been pushed to do so, and that because of this baby, I could stop the treadmill I was on and eliminate the pressure I had learned to live with. What they didn't know was I was comfortable on that treadmill.

Was I supposed to be defined solely as a mother now that I had a baby? I truly wanted to feel like, and be considered, a mother, but that wasn't all I wanted to be. People started saying, "Isn't this the best role you've ever played?" and I'd think, No. First of all, this is not a role I am playing, it's real life, and second, I haven't even begun to tap into my talent as an actress and therefore am hardly ready to retire. Many of the working mothers I knew had given up their careers to be full-time moms and were relieved to do so, but it never occurred to me that I would want to do the same. Even though I'd had a child, I never thought I would have to choose between acting and being a mom. The prospect made me weak. Maybe they weren't insinuating that I had to pack up my acting bags, but they had obviously hit a sore spot. I began to ponder who I was and the ways I had learned to define myself.

Up until now, I realized, I had equated my worth with my successes in my career and at school. Who I was in my own mind was defined only in those arenas. My self-image was directly proportionate to the work I did, and because I worked nonstop, I had little opportunity to cultivate a sense of self separate from the one I held through my profession. I felt strong when I worked, and at ease in my environment. Without my work to rely on, I felt unmoored.

On top of it all, it was my birthday in two days, and I should have been happy, because I supposedly had received the greatest gift in the world. Even though I had been diligently taking the medicine, I wasn't feeling significantly different and kept waiting for it to start working. Chris would be gone on my birthday, so before leaving, he made me promise I would get out of the house on my birthday and have dinner with some close friends.

On my birthday, my mother said she would be thrilled to babysit so I could go to dinner. It was a good sign to her that I wanted to go out at all. I kept my birthday promise to Chris, and on May 31, I wiggled my body into a stretchy dress and went to dinner around the corner with my friends Clarissa and Lyda. I honestly was not ready to see any more people than that and was pleased it was such an intimate gathering. In Lyda's toast, she highlighted the fact that we had been at each other's first birthday parties. Here we sat, after all this time and so many life changes. It made me feel homesick, but I wasn't sure for what. Normally I would've been sad but okay with Chris being in Los Angeles on my birthday, but it was especially difficult for this one. To top it off, I wouldn't be getting a phone call from my father wishing me a happy birthday, and my friend David wasn't around to make fun of me. These two men had been important to me, and without them, I felt unsettled. Why couldn't I shake any of these emotions? What had happened to me? I called Diana the next morning and told her that I wanted to go back in time, before my loved ones had died and before I had challenged my life by having a child. I was afraid I was incapable of being a good mother and that I would never again feel free or happy.

Diana talked about how many people don't connect immediately to their babies; she said that I was overwhelmed and exhausted. She wouldn't get off the phone until I promised her I'd get a baby nurse, even just for a little while. If I could get some more rest, I'd feel a great deal better. Sometimes, she pointed out, it's preferable not to rely on a family member and to hire someone you don't know, someone with whom you have no relationship. It might be easier without history or family baggage to deal with. I still didn't believe that getting help would change how I was feeling, but she insisted that what I was experiencing was too much for anybody to deal with alone. I knew my defenses were down, but I was still having a hard time adapting to the idea of having someone other than family helping out in my home.

Diana said I needed to be able to ask for help without feeling guilty. I'd always had this idea that women should be able to mother their children without help, but this was probably just another one of my idealized notions of motherhood. I realized that many of the women I had known who didn't have baby nurses had extended families who actively helped. Or they were part of cultures in which mothers were allowed to heal and rest before assuming full parental responsibility. After listening to the reasons why I should hire help, I finally acquiesced and decided to make that call; coincidentally, both Lyda and Diana had given me the name and phone number of the same agency.

That night I told my mother about my decision, and I could tell she wasn't thrilled. Maybe she wanted to be given the job herself, or maybe she was concerned for my privacy. My mother hadn't had any help when I was born and hadn't even lived with my father from the time I was five months old, so her idea of mothering was quite different. She had been my sole caregiver, and she never believed in even having a babysitter. She was with me 24/7 and never would have allowed me to spend any amount of time in the care of a relative stranger.

Like many mothers (including me), she wanted to be needed, and she thought that bringing a paid stranger into my home did not seem necessary. Maybe she thought that hiring a baby nurse meant I didn't value her opinions or her help. The truth was that this job was already so fraught with emotion and difficulties that it would be too much for anyone other than a professional. I needed help, and I would have to overlook the fact that my own mother was insulted. The next morning I phoned the agency and asked if they had someone available who could help out for a week. After that, Chris would come back, and then our plan was to take the baby to Los Angeles. Together. We didn't want to be apart from each other for too long. He would return to New York City for just one day to pick us up so I wouldn't have to travel across the country in my current condition alone with a newborn. Chris was relieved that I would be getting help while he was gone, and figured that after a week with a baby nurse, I would be rested and happier. We could start fresh in Los Angeles.

When I spoke to the agency, they said there was one baby nurse who happened to be in the neighborhood, and she could stop by for an interview. I vaguely heard her first name but never even asked for her last name. I quickly agreed to have her come by. Roughly half an hour later, after staring at the door like a dog waiting for her master, I met Gemma.

She was a small woman from the Philippines, about my age, and she smelled very clean, as if she had just bathed with Johnson's shampoo and Ivory soap. I realized it was some sort of perfume, because when I told her she smelled good, she responded, "Oh, today is my day off, but I never wear fragrance around the babies." I hadn't intended it to be a judgment and didn't know how to respond. It hadn't occurred to me that fragrance might be a bad thing for a nanny to wear. (Yet another example of what an inept mother I was.) I quietly led her into the apartment.

My mother was there, too, but said it would be best if I asked the questions. We all sat down in the living room, and at first I couldn't speak. After a few moments and a lot of shifting around, I stupidly asked if Gemma "worked with infants." I could tell she thought it was a dumb question and that I was either drunk or not too intelligent. Trying to analyze my situation and keep some kind of dialogue going, she humored me with an answer.

"Yes, and I have worked for this agency for seven years. I have a thirteen-year-old son, and we live in Queens. I mostly work with infants and newborns but usually not with twins or children much older than two."

"Are you a nurse?" Obviously I had not registered that the title "baby nurse" probably meant that this woman was in fact a nurse who worked with babies!

Gemma smiled and nodded. "Yes."

I was silent. I couldn't think of another thing to ask.

Gemma broke the uncomfortable silence. "So, would you like to ask me any other questions?"

I hung my head and shook it while mumbling, "No."

"Would you like to see my résumé or talk to any of my references?"

I shook my head again, silently, then looked at her and said, "Can you start now?"

"Well, no, but I can get some things from home and return tomorrow morning."

My expression must have been one of horror, because when Gemma looked at me, she seemed to understand that I was having a hard time. She added, "Will you be okay until then?"

Tomorrow seemed like years away, but I was too ashamed to admit my fear of having to cope with the many hours between now and then. I so wished that this stranger, whose last name I still didn't know, would never leave my apartment and would make everything okay immediately. I had made a 180-degree turn from not wanting an unfamiliar person in my house to dreading her departure. I repeated the question in my head. Would I be okay until her return? What could I say?

"Sure. What time will you come back?"

"I'll be here at eight o'clock tomorrow morning."

Oh, how I wished she meant eight P.M. that same day! I said that would be fine, and I thanked her for stopping by. My mother had been equally reticent. Her only contribution was the story of the time we visited Manila in the 1980s. Mom said the nanny was young but seemed sweet, and if I really thought I needed to pay someone to help me, then Gemma would be fine.

My sister had been right. Family brings with it too much pressure.

After a long night, morning finally came. The doorbell rang and relief entered. In walked this little powerhouse of compassion and organization. The first thing she said was "I'll take the baby, you take a shower and get into bed, and I will bring her to you at feeding time." (Yay! Another shower, and I didn't have to sneak it.) This time I took a quick shower and fell immediately asleep. When she brought the baby to me over an hour later, she had given Rowan a sponge bath and changed her clothes. How she managed with the harness, I'll never know. She discussed getting Rowan on a schedule, and did I mind pumping so that she could do an evening feed while I slept?

"When will you sleep?" I asked.

"I don't need much sleep," she replied, and I didn't argue. In the daytime she encouraged me to eat, and gave me big bowls of yogurt and cereal and hot liquids to help with my milk production. Somehow I had missed the part where the baby books talked about needing to eat and drink a lot in order to produce a sufficient quantity of milk. I was beginning to wonder if I ever really read those books; I seemed to have missed every important bit of information in them. I wasn't hungry but saw a big difference in the amount of milk I produced after being reminded to eat. It occurred to me that Gemma's real title should have been "mommy nurse." I began talking to her about my feelings and fears, and she listened. I felt so comfortable around her and loved it when she naturally began calling me by my nickname, "Brookie." Only my family called me this.

Gemma was calming to be around, and I noticed a difference even in Rowan's body language when she was near. Gemma never tried to replace me, but she encouraged the baby and me to become more bonded. Gemma would interpret Rowan's behaviors and said that I would soon be able to tell what my baby needed by the sound of her cry. I told her I wouldn't ever be able to figure that out and that I was a horrible mother. Gemma scoffed. She was always in motion, doing something for Rowan, but when I told her how I felt disconnected to my daughter, she stopped immediately, tilted her head slightly, and looked right into my eyes. At first I got a bit nervous, because her look was so direct, and she obviously had a strong point to make. After a moment of not saying anything, and after she was sure she had my attention, she said her piece.

"Come on, Brookie, you are a very present mother and not like a lot of the 'Hi, bye' moms of today. You are here all the time, and you are the only mother she has. She knows this. She is very alert and strong. It is a big change in your life, and a C-section is a big surgery. You must take it slowly. We will get Sweetie Pie here on a schedule and help you feel strong, and it will all be better."

Somehow, hearing the opinions of this unbiased person made me relax. I didn't resent her views, nor did I feel she was preaching. She had a subtle way of instructing and encouraging. She was never overbearing and managed to help me feel like I was in control and handling it all well. In just a few days, she got Rowan and me on a schedule and infused our lives with a sense of order. She taught me how to bathe Rowan and pat her to sleep when she fussed. When Rowan cried at my breast or wouldn't nurse, Gemma would get down to her level and say, "Sssshhhh, Mommy is right here, and she has everything you need. Momma's gonna feed you, but you have to help her out. Sssshhhh, relax."

Like magic, Rowan would quiet down and latch right on, looking so much like little Nemo from the Disney movie *Finding Nemo* that it soon became another of her nicknames. It was the first time I really saw Rowan's little face looking up at me, and it practically took my breath away. My hair wasn't exactly cascading down, and neither did I feel total peace, but a moment like this gave me hope. I actually looked forward to learning more. It was good to be taught by somebody with whom I felt uninhibited. I was more receptive around Gemma and did not feel judged at all if I didn't know how to do something. In addition, it felt good to be able to talk to someone with whom I didn't have a history. Gemma was tireless, loving, and had a great sense of humor. She didn't belittle my feelings, and she didn't act alarmed by my more gloomy disclosures. I told her about wanting to jump out of the window and running away. I even shared my thoughts about terrible things happening to my little girl. Gemma kept reminding me that having a baby was traumatic, that a C-section was a big deal, and that I needed to be easier on myself. Gemma often said things that made me laugh, and she cooked dinner almost every night. She made foods like grilled salmon or chicken and spinach lasagna and one day even got me to eat fish shell soup to help keep my milk flowing. She said they ate things like fish soup all the time in her hometown, but because it wasn't exactly my favorite, I reminded her that we were not actually in the Philippines and that this was Manhattan! Getting back a bit of my dark sense of humor, I joked that what she was really doing was trying to kill me and take away my baby. I also teasingly accused her of breast-feeding my daughter while I wasn't looking, and made reference to the movie *The Hand That Rocks the Cradle* whenever she took the baby into the other room. I hadn't laughed in so long, and even though I still felt a deep heaviness in my heart, I stopped crying as much. Maybe the medicine was helping a bit. I called my sister to thank her and said the nanny was working out better than I had thought she would.

I knew I needed to stay on this path. I realized that although Gemma was compassionate and smart, she was not a therapist, and I still had many emotions to sort through. I was beginning to recognize that not only did I need medicine and someone to teach me how to care for the baby, I also needed to talk to a professional. Every quiet moment was still filled with dread, and I was sure that all the horrible feelings were going to come flooding back. I decided that once we were back in California, I would find a good therapist.

Chris was so concerned that he called from the West Coast every few hours and was relieved to hear that I seemed to be on a better track. "Are you feeling closer to Rowan?" he'd ask, but I still couldn't affirm that bond. Still feeling sensitive and worried about my relationship with my daughter, I defensively told him not to pressure me and that I was doing the best I could. He stopped asking.

A few days after Gemma's arrival, I got a call from a formula company called Bright Beginnings. They were interested in meeting to discuss the possibility of my endorsing their product. I hadn't planned on using formula but thought it might be a good option as a supplement. I was buoyed by the thought of working in any capacity and said I'd take the meeting. It was the first time in a while that I had to get ready for a professional meeting, and not looking or feeling my best made it a great deal harder. It was difficult figuring out what to put on a body that had been existing only in baggy shirts and my husband's old shorts, but I found something in the "maternity section" of my closet that wasn't a muumuu. I was worried I'd leak through my bra during the meeting, and I knew that would not be an attractive attribute from the point of view of a formula company. But come to think of it, it might have offered visible proof of one of the more positive aspects of bottle-feeding.

I got myself together and took a cab uptown with Gemma and the baby. Gemma took Sweetie Pie on a walk around the office building as I sat down with the Bright Beginnings team and my agent at the time. They put me at the head of a huge oval table in a long boardroom surrounded by big windows. The owner/president of the company and his CEO were on one side, with a representative from the ad agency, a doctor, and the creative director on the other. My agent positioned himself at the far side of the table. I was the only one not in a suit, but there were at least two other women in the meeting, so I wasn't completely outnumbered.

At first it was a bit awkward because it all felt so formal, but soon everyone had introduced themselves to me, and we were having a sweet conversation about family. Daunting as they might sound, these types of meetings never ruffle me, because I have been going to them since I was quite young. There is always a lot of pressure, yet I always manage to stay cool. But in this particular room, at this particular time in my life, I was anything but on my professional game. As I sat at that conference table and looked at those pleasant, accomplished faces and talked about my life as a new mother, I began to cry. I was mortified. I was simply explaining what an adjustment motherhood was and how young my baby was when tears filled my eyes. They came out of the blue, and I just stopped speaking and tilted my head down. I could not control my emotions. Everyone was so sweet to the emotional wreck they were asking to represent their product, and two people offered me tissues. One woman who had kids said, "Yeah, it's tough, isn't it? But it gets so much better." The owner of the company offered up a story about how hard it was for his own wife with their first child, but now they had three children. The whole thing was so embarrassing.

I tried to swallow my emotions as best I could so the meeting could continue. I knew they would never want me as their spokesperson if I couldn't handle even a meeting. They needed a confident, capable role-model mother who was bonded to her child. I surely didn't fit the bill! I was a chubby, blubbering idiot who cried in front of strangers at serious business meetings. I successfully reined in my emotions and, apologizing, took the tissue, cleared my throat, and continued to discuss my views on nursing.

They kept reiterating that "breast is and always will be best," but that not everyone can or chooses to breast-feed. I had many reservations about formula and never would have considered using it had I not met this team of professionals. They insisted that they did not expect me to use only formula, but if Rowan liked Bright Beginnings, and if I was willing to use it as a supplement, then we would have a good relationship. They suggested I talk to my doctor to feel better about introducing formula and then call them. They said all the right things to make me feel secure about the benefits of their product, and I wouldn't have to stop breast-feeding, either. We continued to discuss the positive effects of their product, and they gave me a can to take home. I left the meeting and then went to discuss it all with my agent. The minute we could speak privately, he exclaimed, "Great job on the crying!"

I couldn't believe my ears. "What?" I said.

"Yeah, that really sent it home, and they were blown away by you."

I wanted to throw up. After I regained my composure, I explained that I had not been faking it. I didn't want to get into a discussion about how pathetic and distasteful it would be for me to use tears and my daughter to win people over. I stuck to business and explained some of my terms if the deal were to go through. I would not allow my daughter to be in any ads, but if she liked the product, and if I could use it only as a supplement and not as a substitute for nursing, I would be happy to work with the company.

I left the building feeling like I had just been in an accident.

It surprised me that stepping back into my professional life, even for a short time, had been harder than I thought. Back at the apartment, I decided to wait a bit before giving Rowan the formula. I discussed it at length with Chris and Gemma, who both said that it depended on how I felt about it. I did not want to stop breast-feeding but thought it might not hurt to have a backup. Chris agreed that it would be a nice safety net to have a good supplement. I was also extremely worried that if Rowan did like the formula, then she would no longer want the real thing. Gemma assured me that the baby wouldn't reject me; I never asked how she knew that for sure, but I trusted her not to lead me astray. She said that Rowan was now so comfortable with me that it wouldn't threaten our bond whatsoever. She had proven to be fine on a bottle with pumped milk and hadn't rejected me. If I wanted to have a formula as a resource, I should try it.

A few days later, I took the plunge. I put some ready-made formula in Rowan's bottle, warmed it up, and gave it to her. She gobbled it down without complaining a bit. It was as if she had only ever been on formula. What had I done? Now I was sure she wouldn't want me anymore! I panicked and considered calling my agent and saying she hated it and I couldn't take the job. Paranoia coursed through my veins, and I was convinced I had ruined all the progress I had made in trying to breast-feed. I had undermined my own plan all because I was greedy to work again. I felt myself spiral out of control once more.

Gemma intervened and, peeling me off of the ceiling, said I didn't need to worry. The baby would not reject me. She was adaptable, and we would start slowly. Plus, if I couldn't pump sufficiently for some reason, the formula would provide another opportunity for Chris to give her a bottle. It wouldn't hurt to be as prepared as possible. Rowan had already gotten the colostrum and the important antibodies. A bit of formula wouldn't hurt. I could take the job and probably regain some of my self-confidence from working. Gemma added, "It would also be good for the baby to feel you happier and strong." I didn't know how this woman could have insight into my emotions, but I didn't question her. I signed on to be the spokesperson but luckily wouldn't have to do the commercial for at least a few months. I would be able to continue breast-feeding for a long time and supplement with the formula when I chose to.

Chris returned to New York, and we prepared for our return to L.A. I called Dr. Rebarber in his New York office and informed him that I was getting ready to go back to L.A. and that I had gotten a nanny and was feeling a bit better. I added that because I didn't think the medicine was really working, I was going to stop taking it. When I finished my little speech, he laughed and said, "Trust me, it's working." He suggested that I take it for a while longer, and after I had settled down in L.A., we could discuss my going off of it. I told him I didn't want to need it, and he repeated that it wasn't addictive and that I wouldn't have to be on it for long. "Let's just be patient," he said. Ugh! That dreaded word again. I wanted to prove to myself that I could get better without help. Even though I had friends and family who were taking antidepressant medication and it was helping them, and I knew that taking it truly wasn't a terrible thing, I still wanted to believe I could feel better on my own. I remember being told that, even as a little girl, my favorite thing to say was "Do it myself, do it myself!" Some things never change. Begrudgingly, however, I agreed to keep taking the drug.

I was terrified to leave Gemma. In the end, it was probably a good idea not to go off the medicine at the same time I was leaving my Tita support system. "Tita" means aunt in Tagalog, and I had started calling Gemma this name as a term of endearment. Chris and I didn't have a firm plan in place for when we were in L.A. but were hoping to find some type of help once we got there. I'll never forget driving away from my Filipino soul sister standing on the New York street, waving goodbye, and crying. Athough it had been only a little over a week, so much had transpired, and a friendship had blossomed. I was afraid that all the old bad stuff would return without her to talk me down.

On the way to the airport, Chris told me emphatically not to worry and that I would be fine. I stared out of the window and honestly wasn't sure I could do it without Gemma. I explained my fear openly and with a great deal of emotion, and I could tell Chris thought I was being a bit dramatic. After all, Gemma and I had been together only a short time. Chris looked at me with a slightly worried expression and asked if I had gone off of my medicine. I don't blame him for being concerned about my mental state, but I got very insulted. I looked in his eyes and saw concern and a certain wariness. Why did even my husband want me medicated? Was I really that unstable? Trust seemed to be an issue, and I feared that the people close to me would never trust me to be whole or completely sane again. I answered with a curt "No." Chris added that I wouldn't have to be on the medicine forever, but it did seem like it was helping, and why not take advantage of it?

I kept repeating that I wanted to be happy again—with our baby, with motherhood, and with life in general. I couldn't understand why this was happening to me. Chris touched my hand and said he firmly believed that these bad feelings were temporary and that he not only wanted me to be happy, he believed I would feel better with time. He said I shouldn't be afraid or embarrassed to take medicine, and it was not a terrible thing to accept all the help that was available. I should get better, and then we could discuss the medicine. I felt ashamed to even be having this conversation with him. I remained shocked that I couldn't be happier on my own. Every other time in my life when things were tough, I had proved to myself that I could weather the storm and be okay on my own. This was the first time I had needed help. I returned to staring out of the window as Rowan slept peacefully, and just said, "I'm sorry."

"Don't be, honey, we'll get through this." Thank God he was so understanding. I know I wouldn't have been able to continue if he'd been any less patient. One of us had to possess this needed quality. I put Rowan in the BabyBjörn as we journeyed through the airport. I heard congratulations from so many strangers and wondered if they would be saying that if they knew what was actually going on.

On the plane, a very interesting thing happened. Sitting next to us were Kate Lear and her husband, Jonathan LaPook, who were friends of other people we knew on the same flight. All I knew about Kate was that she was the daughter of Norman Lear. We all introduced ourselves, and everyone marveled at how beautiful our daughter was. Jonathan is a doctor, and he kept looking at me with a warm yet inquisitive expression. He asked me a few times how I was, and I remember thinking, Did someone put a sign on my forehead that says, Not doing well? I said, "Fine," but each time he pressed on like a heat-seeking missile. Suddenly he volunteered the information that his wife had had a hard time after their first child was born. We hadn't exactly brought up the subject, and this comment seemed to come out of the blue. I was a bit taken aback. Was this a sign? Of all the people to be flying with, we get a doctor and his smart, successful wife who, we were to learn, had battled a post natal anxiety disorder for almost two years.

Not at my suggestion, they switched seats, and Kate told me her story. She described what those first few months were like for her after childbirth and how they had changed her life. She told me she'd never had any experience with a mood disorder and had been so shocked by it that she had even written an article about it. She said she would send it to me as soon as she got home. I had very little to add to the conversation, but it was interesting, so I tuned in. At first I couldn't believe it had been that bad for her, but as she spoke, she was very serious. She talked about her insomnia and about feeling pathetic. It became clear how grave her situation had been. Both Chris and I listened. The things she was saying started to sound familiar. Here was an articulate, talented woman who was painting a picture that was similar to my own. She mentioned the terrible anxiety she had experienced, as well as the alarming mood swings. She had no appetite, would wander around her home waiting for sunrise, and felt as if she wasn't herself. The point she kept repeating was that "nobody talks about it, and they should. It can be debilitating."

Even though I could identify with some of what she was saying, I still couldn't bring myself to admit that maybe I was experiencing post natal depression. She was not at all intrusive; she was very warm and quite open. Plus, she had her son with her, and he seemed close to his mom. After a little while, it was time to feed Rowan, so I excused myself. As Rowan suckled away, I silently tried to picture what Kate had gone through. I kept hearing some of her words in my head, like "self-doubt" and "panic." I started thinking it was possible that I, too, was going through something serious. Maybe it was more common than I had thought. I started to wonder if this meeting had happened for a reason.

It was obvious that I needed to become further informed. I have always believed in the adage "Knowledge is power," and maybe with enough information, I could garner the power necessary to get through this torture. Upon deplaning, Chris suggested we keep in touch, and I suggested we all get sent to a mental institution together. It wasn't at all funny, and I regretted saying it. I meant no disrespect but felt like I was in some kind of intervention and was being forced to admit I had a disease. Once we got to our house in Los Angeles, I decided I'd take a serious look at the material my friend Sherie had given me on this so-called affliction, post natal depression.

CHAPTER 5

HAD A GREAT FALL

Even though I was still feeling pretty bad, I believed that all I needed was a change of scenery. Maybe the Los Angeles weather would improve my mood and I would begin to feel better soon. I would forget the past few weeks and start over. The environment there was much more serene than in New York. Although I will forever call New York City home, and I prefer being there over anywhere else, it does have a tendency to be crowded and loud. At night we hear fire trucks and sirens and all the delivery vehicles noisily traveling across town. Needless to say, sleeping is more difficult, and the environment is not always conducive to feeling centered. Where we live in L.A. is incredibly peaceful. I couldn't wait to settle into the house and to start experiencing the constant sunshine. I looked forward to establishing the same schedule we'd had in New

York, which had been working well. I was exhausted after the flight, and my mind was reeling from our encounter with Kate Lear. I was too tired to read the material on post natal depression and decided I would do so when I was more rested.

Unlike in New York, where friends can drop by easily, in Los Angeles you have to drive everywhere. Therefore, it's hard to get help from friends, because people don't live close to one another, and it's impossible to get around quickly. In addition, none of our family lived there, either, so we felt a bit isolated and thought we could use some assistance sooner rather than later. It was a new environment for Rowan, and I was worried she might feel unsettled. I had no doubt she'd be affected by the time change, and I wanted to make sure I had help available in case she had trouble adjusting. So Chris and I decided to hire another baby nurse for one week, to help us get situated.

I assumed we would find someone similar to Gemma. We called the agency in New York, and they had a baby nurse available on the West Coast. I couldn't believe how easy it was to hire her. The new woman met us at our house, and within ten minutes it became clear that she was the antithesis of Gemma. She had a drastically different, old-school approach to caretaking, and I felt as if I had been transported back to another era. She wore a nurse's uniform and called me "ma'am." She prefaced everything with "Well, with my babies I prefer to . . ." She held Rowan like a football and would put the baby over her knee, facedown, and bounce her up and down while looking out of the window, watching TV, or singing songs I didn't recognize. I got the feeling she expected me to ring some sort of bell to call her, hand over the baby, and then go entertain guests! I was looking for a set of helping hands rather than a primary caretaker. No matter how bad I felt, even in New York, I had remained committed to being a hands-on mom. This woman was a competent baby nurse but was not used to working for mothers who spent time around their babies. She seemed surprised that I was always there. Under Gemma's calming and nonintrusive tutelage, I had gotten used to doing things a certain way, and this woman had a different approach to every area of child care. It was a frustrating situation for both of us.

Rowan had jet lag and seemed unsettled around this new person. I knew it was important for me to be well rested, so I decided to pump some milk so the baby nurse could give Rowan the three A.M. feedings and I could sleep. Six A.M. always came too quickly, and because of my mixed feelings about the baby nurse, I'd had trouble sleeping. I wasn't able to catch up on my rest, and I was beginning to feel unnerved once again. I wouldn't leave my baby with the nurse and instead began taking her with me everywhere. I started making excuses to justify why I had to bring Rowan with me. I'd leave the house, yelling out that I needed to take her to a doctor's appointment or that we were going to a playdate. Rowan was quite young for playdates and it was rather ridiculous, I know, but the end result was that I surprised myself with my competency. Rowan and I went all over L.A., and even with her harness on, I got used to putting her in the BabyBjörn or the stroller with one hand. It felt like a triumph to be able to navigate the car seat and all of the other things one needs when one has a child. The fact that I was mastering the logistics all by myself made me feel more confident.

Funny but annoying things started to happen during the long week the nurse was in our house. For example, once when Chris and

I were leaving with the baby, she said, "Oh, would you bring me back some salmon?" I guess she was used to a different kind of household, one with servants and a chef. We had neither a chef nor any type of house staff except a cleaning lady who came for a few hours twice a week. We did the grocery shopping and cooking ourselves. Well, Chris is really the chef in the house. Contrary to what people might think, we are rather low-key. Except for the time with Gemma in New York, I have never had live-in help. This woman didn't live in California, so she had to stay with us. It was weird seeing someone I had just met standing in front of my open fridge in her nightgown.

On our way to the market, Chris and I laughed, made fun of her request, and then got the salmon. The next morning we started joking that we couldn't stay at the dog park too long because we had to return home and cook the nanny breakfast. Chris would say that he couldn't go on a walk with the baby and me because he needed to stay at home and make sure the nanny's champagne was chilled and the Jacuzzi was heated. We had committed to the week with her, and did want a nurse in the house just in case anything went awry, but I began counting the days until Wrong Nanny was gone. We felt like we were living someone else's life. It did, however, feel great to be able to laugh at our situation, and it indicated to me and my husband that my mood was indeed improving.

I thought it was a good sign that I had strong opinions about Rowan's care, because at the very least, it highlighted the fact that I was more engaged with her life and with motherhood in general. I even began to recognize some of Rowan's patterns of behavior, which I took as another positive sign. I began to know when she was tired versus when she was hungry or bored. I could anticipate when she was about to fall asleep without finishing nursing: Her big eyes would start to roll back, and I'd have to lightly touch her cheek so she'd continue to drink. If I didn't intervene fast enough, she'd fall asleep too deeply and I wouldn't be able to stir her. Gemma had been right; I could tell Rowan's mood by the tone or cadence of her cry. I was learning to bond with my daughter from the outside in, and although it was a slow process, I felt less hopeless. I don't know if it had anything to do with the fact that, as I'd promised my doctor, I'd been diligently taking that little pink pill, but I was no longer crying morning 'til night.

Rowan's presence still scared me. She was a huge responsibility, and I wasn't sure I was completely qualified for the job. Marriage is a commitment, but at least my husband can feed himself and go to the bathroom on his own! For my work in various roles, I had undergone intensive training of my voice and body, but nothing could have prepared me for the rigors of motherhood. Rowan came without a call sheet or stage directions. Every day I joked about meeting her for the first time, because I felt as if I still didn't really know her. I worried that I was alienated from her; I had hoped by this point things would be different. Nonetheless, Rowan got cuter the more I stared at her. She was a very happy baby and had a sweetness to her that I was beginning to appreciate. Our week with the baby nurse finally ended, and Chris and I had never been happier to see someone leave our house.

I still hadn't followed up on reading the material about post natal depression and confessed to Chris that I was avoiding it for some reason. I knew the information would be troubling, and I continued to feel that it couldn't possibly pertain to me. Chris had said that it would be helpful to hear other people's stories, but he didn't pressure me. I could tell he was disappointed, so I reassured him that I would eventually get around to it. Over the past few weeks, I had been thinking more clearly, and my emotions were more level. I hadn't considered jumping out a window or running away, and I was no longer consumed by misery. I believed I was getting my feelings under control, and I didn't want anything else to make me feel bad. I couldn't imagine that reading the literature would be a barrel of laughs. Things in general were appearing less dark and not as overwhelming as they had been in New York City. I wanted only to keep feeling happier and to avoid rocking the boat in which I was now floating. Time seemed to pass more quickly and with much less drama.

Before I knew it, we needed to focus on a photo shoot for *HELLO!* magazine. In another attempt to preempt the media, we had decided long before Rowan was born to work with this UK publication because they had been kind to me in the past. I would be able to have photo approval, and it would (hopefully) be a non-gossipy article. After the story appeared, there would no longer be a desire for "The first-ever-to-be-released photos of baby Rowan at home!" If we were proactive, we knew we'd be less hunted by the hungry, invasive photo hounds. I wanted to lessen the appeal in any way I could, and hopefully afterward we could all go about our lives less disturbed. There would, of course, always be the parasitic paparazzi taking shots of us from behind various bushes in the neighborhood when we went on our walks, but with our story out quickly, those pictures would have less market value.

When Chris and I had arranged the shoot, we never thought

I would have any problems after the birth. Now Chris was worried I would have a hard time doing it, and I could tell he wished we hadn't set it up. He told me that in light of all that had happened with me, maybe it was now not a good idea. He is a very private person and felt weird posing along with our baby for photos that would be distributed nationally. Again I explained that we didn't have much of a choice. Chris has never had to deal with such issues in his own life, and when it comes to being in the public eye, he usually takes my lead. I recalled how well it had gone when we left the hospital, and although I did strongly resent even having to think about these things, I wanted to be in charge of as much of it as I could. We would not be able to stop pictures from being taken and put in the press, so we might as well have a modicum of control. This way we could at least pick the images we wanted and present a story with which we felt comfortable. I don't usually take professional photos of any kind in our home, but in this case I made an exception because I knew the baby would feel more at ease there.

Ever since I was a little girl, I've worked on photo shoots. I grew up thinking of certain photographers and people on the set as members of my extended family. Consequently, photo shoots never make me nervous, and because I was feeling better, I wasn't feeling stressed out about this one at all. It would also be wonderful at this early stage of Rowan's life to have beautiful pictures of the whole family. We wouldn't regret it. When the day arrived and the team of people showed up, I was actually excited. This would be a little taste of the work I had been craving since Rowan was born, and it might even be fun. As a child, I often got lost in the dream world of photo taking. Whenever I was in front of the camera, it felt like I was escaping from my life, and any problems I had would temporarily be forgotten. In my current state, I welcomed such a distraction.

I knew the pictures would be special because we had a terrific photographer shooting them. I picked out some adorable outfits for my little girl to wear and reveled in the fact that I felt proud to show her off. What a relief to be experiencing such an emotion after the past weeks of gloom! Maybe I was finally snapping out of it. I was thankful for the opportunity to document my growing family. In a strange way, I also hoped that if I really looked happy and bonded with my baby in the pictures, that would help me believe it was true. Any therapist would have a field day with my interpretation, but whether it is a good thing or not, photography does play a role in my life. I knew that seeing happy, pretty photos of me and my daughter would help me to focus on the good that did exist.

The shoot went well, and we had fun. Chris, who doesn't enjoy being photographed and usually does a funny thing with his mouth in photos, started off uncomfortable but soon relaxed. The lights and the action fascinated Rowan. She never cried and wasn't at all scared. I would have felt horrible if she had been upset by the activity for which I was responsible. The small crew was lovely and gentle and incredibly thoughtful with Rowan. They were soft-spoken and sensitive to her feeding schedule and mood. I didn't remember people ever being that thoughtful on a photo shoot and was pleasantly surprised. Chris was so amused by our daughter's many expressions. After the day was over, we all had a nice dinner together while Rowan passed out on my chest. It was the first time I got a glimpse of what my life could be like as a working mom. I didn't want to make photo shoots a habit for my daughter, but selfishly, I felt a bit less isolated from my old life.

The pictures turned out even better than we had expected, and the response we got from the article was incredible. Everyone commented on how happy I looked and how beautiful Rowan was. Many friends asked for the photographer's name so they could have pictures taken of their own families. When I saw the layout, I was struck by how peaceful I looked. And what a happy family! At last I was seeing the picture that had been etched in my mind so long ago. The best part about the shoot was that it never felt false or like an act, so there must have been some truth to the emotions evident in the pictures. I decided to display the photos around the house to remind me, should I start to feel down again, of the connection I really did have to my daughter and to my life.

While in Los Angeles, I called Gemma often for advice. Even though I didn't yet feel deeply connected to Rowan, and I wondered if the bad feelings would return and destroy the peace, my daughter was becoming more of a welcome new roommate. She seemed to be growing daily. She smiled at anybody who came to visit and was even starting to make giggling sounds when tickled. Because Chris was getting home from work too late at night, he could spend time with Rowan only in the mornings. She loved the regularity of her routine, and the times I did try to keep her up past her bedtime so her dad could see her, she had a meltdown and then was very hard to put to sleep.

I had assumed that, once I was settled in L.A., I could stop the medicine. So, because the days were passing more smoothly, I decided that I had been on Paxil long enough and stopped taking it.

I didn't call my doctor in New York because it didn't seem necessary. I felt it was no big deal—I would call him later to tell him what I'd done and that I was fine. I didn't wean myself or tell anyone I was going off the medicine. I just went off it cold turkey. I didn't even tell Chris, because I knew he would object, and deep down, I did not want to be told to stay on it. Stubbornly, I believed I'd be okay. I had always been a big believer in mind over matter, so I thought I was now strong enough, and sufficiently well rested, to will myself into feeling better. After stopping Paxil, I felt no immediate change in my mood and believed I was adjusting well to my new role as mom. Obviously I was ready to go it alone, without drugs.

A few nights after going off the medicine, I decided to go back to the *Suddenly Susan* lot to visit some friends from the crew. Ironically, they were all working on Chris's show now. I had spent four years with this team, and I knew they'd be thrilled to meet my little girl. I walked into the wardrobe department, and people immediately started taking turns holding the tiny bundle. We took Polaroids, and I told them the dramatic story about Rowan's birth. It was such a familiar environment that I felt like I had returned home. As I started reminiscing with them about our time together filming *Suddenly Susan* and how much fun we'd had, I started to get weepy. Because they were in the middle of taping an episode, there was a lot going on. Actors and other people were coming in and out of the room to change costumes. As I watched all this activity, I started feeling like I was moving further and further away from everybody. The sadness I felt had a certain momentum to it, and I got rather worked up. I looked at these people who had been like a family to me, and I missed being in their environment. I felt left out.

Working in TV, in film, or on Broadway is all-consuming. Your world basically revolves around the work and the relationships in the workplace. There isn't time for much else. If and when the job ends, it's like losing your home and your family. For years I was intimately bonded with these people, but everyone had understandably moved on to other jobs and other "families." I, too, had moved on to create my own family and was currently on the other side of the lens. I began feeling uncomfortable, as if I would never again be accepted as part of this world. I remember once, when I was the new kid in high school (who also happened to be famous!), I brought my lunch tray to a table, and every student sitting there got up and left in unison. I was so hurt. I ended up moving to the teachers' table. Although I was in a very different scenario now, I felt very much the same as I did that day in school.

The costume designer, Judith, and her assistant, Kris, both noticed my uneasy and sad expression. They shut the door behind them so we could have some privacy. Once the four of us were in the room alone, I cried. "I miss you guys. I want it to be like it was before, when we were all together."

Judith was the first to respond: "Believe me, you are not missing a thing! Look at how wonderful that beautiful baby is. She is more important than anything."

"I know, but I don't know where I belong anymore."

Judith looked at me sympathetically. "We all miss you, but we will work together again. For now, you have to be where you are and appreciate it. It's a blessing. Don't be sad, it's all for a reason."

Judith was a Buddist and had a Zen attitude about most things. She never preached or tried to convert people. Her belief was often calming for me in times of stress; when David died, she was able to come to terms with the tragedy long before the rest of us did. I told Judith that I just wanted to come back, but I wasn't sure if I knew where I wanted to come back to. At that moment I wanted to be with them, like a family once more, working and enjoying one another on our TV show. I wanted to go back to a time when I knew what I could expect from myself and I could do it with pride.

Judith tried to remind me of the reality of my life. "You haven't gone anywhere. You just had a baby. It will all work out the way it's meant to."

Suddenly I became self-conscious. I started feeling silly for complaining and pouring my emotions out to her, so I added that I was just being silly and hormonal. "I'm fine. I'm sorry for being such a downer. I just miss the fun we had together and hope to do it again." I fought back my negative thoughts. I shifted the focus back to the baby and gave her some shiny costume jewelry to play with.

Some high-powered executives stopped in to see the baby, and they kept commenting on how great it must be for me to be a mom and not to have to deal with the craziness of the business. I had never thought it was too crazy and had always imagined that I'd continue to work and would just bring my child to the set. People were being kind, and I imagine some would have changed places with me in a second. But I started feeling like I no longer mattered. In their eyes, I was no longer an actress; I was now just a mom. To an actress, this can be quite frightening. Some of the fears I'd had in New York began returning. I got this horrible feeling that I would never work again and that I had not timed having a baby properly (as if you can ever really time a baby). I started wishing I had waited until I was in another full-time job before having a family. After having worked steadily my whole life, here I was without a job. I wasn't earning my own living and I wasn't doing what I had always considered to be my life's work. I wasn't handling my current "job" so well, either. Needless to say, my senses of identity and self had been markedly unsettled.

As people continued to appear in the wardrobe department to get a glimpse of the new baby, I became more and more disoriented. Once again I felt awkward and began panicking. This time it had nothing to do with Rowan but instead had everything to do with how I felt about myself. It felt physical, like I was about to get sick or faint. I couldn't understand what was happening. I had been doing so well. My heart began to race, my hearing became muffled, and I had to get out of there immediately. I stood up and looked at my watch. Scooping up the baby, I gathered our things and said quick goodbyes, all the while pretending that I needed to get Rowan home and into bed because it was getting late. Tapings are done in the evenings, and it was close to her bedtime, but I had originally planned to stay at the set later and let her fall asleep in the car on the way home. I said I would visit again but for now I should let them all get back to work. Walking quickly to my car, I began to cry. I got the baby in the car seat and left the lot as soon as possible. Then the tears flooded down.

I hit traffic on the drive home and starting getting the terrible feeling that I was going to ram the car into the wall on the side of the freeway. The baby was in the back, and though I didn't think of hurting her, I wanted to smash violently through the window myself. Thank God the baby was in the car, because this urge was so strong

that I feared I would actually do it. How ironic that she was saving
me from hurting myself! For a reason I can't explain, I called my
mother. Maybe I hoped she'd make me feel better, or maybe I knew
she would make me feel worse and that I deserved it. Whatever my
crazy reason for calling her first, I did, and I scared the daylights out
of her. She tried calming me down and told me that these feelings
were only temporary. She told me how blessed I was and to keep saying my prayers. She asked if I was still taking the medicine, and I
said, "No!" I told her I had to keep driving and couldn't talk anymore. I hung up leaving her desperately concerned. Later I felt bad
for worrying her so.

Next I phoned my friend Stephanie. We had lived together after
college in New York and Los Angeles and had a long-standing, deep,
sisterlike friendship. I told her I wanted to drive the car into the wall.
I sobbed to her about feeling crazy again. She knew I always kept my
word, so she made me seriously promise I wouldn't do anything rash.
She said it three times. I promised not to, but the desire was overwhelming. Then she said she'd come over if I needed her to. I didn't
want to see anyone at that moment but agreed I would meet her the
next day for lunch. She was relieved that I was even speaking in terms
of a tomorrow. I never called Chris because I didn't want to upset
him at work. Rowan and I finally got home. I was shaking. The baby
went to bed easily, but I cried myself to sleep. I kept thinking how
glad I was that Chris hadn't witnessed my breakdown.

The next morning I sat on the bed and told him about my collapse. He looked broken. He didn't ask for details, he just said, "I
can't take it anymore, please do something to feel better. I never
know when something is going to happen, and I don't know what to

do anymore. I can't stand seeing you like this. Please!" Surprisingly, he didn't ask if I was still taking the medicine. I hadn't thought of it while it was happening, but in reviewing the last few days and last night, I considered the fact that going off the medicine may have contributed to my collapse. When I ashamedly volunteered to my husband that I had gone off of the drug and that I thought my reaction might have been a result of that (and not that I had gone completely insane), he said that whatever it was, I needed to talk to someone who could really help. His focus had shifted from the medicine to my needing serious help.

It had been going so well, and I had seemed so much better. Chris had begun to let his guard down around me; it seemed as if he really thought I was getting stronger and moving past "it." What happened the night before came as a real blow to both of us. He was defenseless. He begged me to go to a hospital or get some kind of help because he couldn't stand my feeling like this any longer. He couldn't live through it. He wasn't being selfish but admitted he was very worried and was losing his ability to stay strong. Sitting on the edge of the bed, he hung his head low and looked sad and defeated. My emotions had taken a toll. His helpless demeanor made me plummet even further. I couldn't believe I was causing such unhappiness, pain, and confusion to the man I loved. What was I doing to my family? I hated myself.

After Chris had left for work, I asked Alma, our cleaning lady, to stay with Rowan while I went to lunch with Stephanie. Not only had Alma been with us for a long time and had two kids of her own, but I trusted her. I had only two hours before the next feeding, so there would be little time for small talk. The moment I sat down with

Steph, I looked at her and said, "I am going crazy. I am not doing well at all." Because we have known each other for about fifteen years, we have seen each other through many ups and downs. She admitted that she had never seen me this upset before. I was desperate and needed to get my mind in order. I kept repeating how scared I was. She talked to me at great length and calmed me down. She helped me see that I wasn't crazy but that there was truly something serious going on inside of me and that it was out of my control. I needed medical help before it got any worse. Stephanie made me focus on, and verbally list, all of the wonderful things in my life and all of my accomplishments. She knew I loved Rowan and that Rowan loved me and that I was going to get past this. She reminded me that there had never been anything I couldn't do once I set my mind to it. This was a test and I would pass it. I told her about the medication, and she made me swear I would call the doctor. I felt like a little kid taking orders. All I could do was give in totally to Steph's advice and compassion. I left lunch feeling a bit better and like I had some extra protection around me. Chris had remained so strong up until now, but it was time for me to reach out for even more help. I didn't want to hurt him any more than I had already.

On my way back home, I thought about how my dear friend David had spiraled out of control. He, too, had gone off of his medication without telling his doctor. I felt even more compassion for him than I had before. Why did I think that I could go off the medicine without seeking medical assistance? Why did I think I would be exempt from the side effects? David and I were obviously in different predicaments, but looking back now, I can't believe I didn't learn more from the gravity of his situation. I understood why he didn't wish to be medicated, but I wonder if he'd still be with us had he stayed on his medication. I lost one of the most important people in my life, and I should have learned then to have more respect for the value of medication.

I went home and tentatively spoke to my assistant about my emotional state. She usually is in her office but that day had some extra work to do at our house. She has a very respectful approach to me and to my life in general and has established her own strict boundaries that she never oversteps. She has worked with me for over seven years and stays behind the scenes. I trust her implicitly. I sat down with her and asked her about my behavior. She looked at me with tears in her eyes and admitted that she had never seen me act like this before. My heart seemed dark, and it hurt her to see me so unhappy and full of rage. We see each other daily, so I asked if she'd noticed whether I had significantly changed in the past few days. She said yes. When I first arrived in Los Angeles, it seemed like I was beginning to adjust to everything and that no problem was too big, but recently I seemed overwhelmed by even the simplest dilemma. I explained that I had stopped taking the medicine prescribed to me. My assistant looked right at me, picked up the phone, and handed it to me with the number of my local gynecologist.

"YOU WENT OFF the Paxil cold turkey? Oh boy, Brooke, no wonder you feel the way you do! Who told you to do that?"

I told her that I'd taken it upon myself to stop taking the medication because I really didn't think it was working.

"Do you still feel the same about it?" she inquired, to which I sheepishly replied, "I guess that's the beauty of a drug like that; you don't even realize it's doing its job, but somehow you feel better." I told her I had hoped I was doing better as a result of mind control and that I didn't want to *need* drugs to feel better. After I'd filled her in on what a tough time I'd had since Rowan's birth, she said it sounded like I was experiencing a more acute form of post natal depression. It's a real affliction, she said, and because for some reason people are hesitant to talk about it, it isn't diagnosed nearly enough. She kindly explained that I didn't need to put the added pressure on myself to endure something that was clearly out of my control. I shouldn't feel ashamed, and I should know that it is much more common than people think. She said she had seen it a lot with women who had gone through IVF (perhaps due to the manipulation of their hormones) but that it can happen to anybody. It was not an indication that I was crazy, or that somehow it was my fault. There were no medals being handed out to people who chose to stay miserable. Medicine existed for a reason. Not treating the illness would be irresponsible.

I remembered someone saying once that you don't always succeed at doing something just because you *decide* to. I was trying to *think* myself into feeling better, and it was obviously not working. Help is there to be taken advantage of, and whatever it took to feel better and regulate my body would be worth it. I suddenly remembered Kate Lear's husband looking at Chris and saying, "Nothin' wrong with better living through medicine." My doctor said that there were many choices of drugs to try, but as long as the medicine I had been taking seemed to be working, I should start by trying it once more. It helped to be reminded that the drug wasn't physically addictive, and that when the time was right I could stop taking it, as long as I did so with a doctor's guidance. That day I started taking the pink pill again.

A few days later, I went in to see my doctor for a checkup and a sonogram. Ever since I had come home from the hospital in New York and had been feeling so bad, I had completely forgotten about the issue with my uterus. Chris and I had been told that we wouldn't know if it had healed entirely until more time had gone by and I had fully recovered. The doctor did a full exam, and we were both relieved to find out that my uterus had gone back to normal and that everything looked fine in the egg factory. She had analyzed my medical record from the delivery, and even though she wasn't sure why any of it had happened in the first place, she wasn't worried that my uterus would become herniated again. She said I could have another child if I chose to, but that the birth would have to be via a scheduled C-section. I responded that I had enough to handle right now. Besides, I was so afraid of going through another depression. She explained that just because post natal depression has happened with one child, it wouldn't necessarily occur after subsequent births. Plus, with the proper preemptive drug protocol, it can be avoided. It is hard to know for sure whether someone is predisposed to PPD, and like many women faced with it, I was shocked that it had happened at all. I found it comforting to hear my doctor say that I couldn't have seen it coming, and that there was no shame in having it. She said there's pressure for women to suppress their feelings, swallow their emotions, and get on with mothering. Perhaps we don't take seriously enough the effect that hormones and other factors can have on our well-being and peace of mind. Sadly, post natal depression has only recently been brought to the public's attention, and most often that attention has focused on the severest of cases. Until now it has remained one of those topics that doesn't get talked about often by those afflicted or by their doctors.

I remained curious about the genesis of my emotions and wondered about the difference between post natal depression and the baby blues. My most recent and quite serious mood swing, and the range and depth of the emotions I had experienced during those first few weeks of Rowan's life, had placed me on what I would consider the verge of insanity. I obviously needed to become more educated about this form of depression. I finally sat down and read the material that Sherie had given me.

Although there doesn't seem to be a consensus as to what causes post natal depression, many believe that the rapid change in hormones at delivery may be significant enough to cause a mood shift. However, in many cases the symptoms actually begin during pregnancy. Other factors believed to contribute to post natal depression include sleep deprivation; a difficult pregnancy; complications at birth for the mother or child; inadequate social support; marital problems; a history of depression; and the recent occurrence of a major life change, such as divorce, death, a new job, or a recent move. The onset is usually within a week after giving birth, but it has been known to occur even up to one year later (for example, when a woman stops breast-feeding and starts menstruating again). It can last anywhere from a few months to a couple of years if left untreated, though it is considered to be post natal depression only if it starts within the first year post natal.

One reason why the diagnosis isn't made more often is because doctors may be more focused on the mother's physical recovery and the newborn's progress and might not ask enough questions about the mother's mental health. In addition, at least some of the symptoms of post natal depression are present in many women after giving birth, which may make it more difficult to diagnose: They may have trouble sleeping or focusing, they may have little energy, their appetite may be off (they're eating too little or too much), and/or they may feel mildly depressed. The diagnosis is easier to make when a woman experiences more extreme mood shifts; if she has a history of depression; or when there has been has an obvious emotional trauma preceding the birth that might foreshadow a consequent problem. Even then some women are reluctant to admit it, and doctors don't always ask the right questions. The scary part is that post natal depression can also occur when no such precipitating event exists.

There seems to be a real stigma surrounding the disease; yet, left undiagnosed, it can be chronic and devastating. The mother may be racked with guilt and ravaged by hopelessness, and the rest of the family is affected as well. Husbands, parents, and children will ultimately suffer, and in some instances whole families may be torn apart. This is a serious illness that needs to be dealt with. Once it has been properly diagnosed, medicine and therapy can provide much of the desired relief.

Had I been a prime candidate? Hindsight is, as usual, 20/20, and once I examined my life more closely, it became clear that the writing had been on the nursery wall. My doctor asked if I had a history of depression, but I had never experienced anything beyond melancholy and the occasional low period that can be a part of life. No emotions ever leveled me the way these did. Usually I could soldier through almost any problem by using my own resources: I could rely on exercise to clear my mind; I could write about my emotions in a diary, take a meditative yoga class, or hike to feel better. Sometimes all I'd need to do was get a full night's sleep or spend some time with a close friend in order to change my perspective on a problem. No matter how sad I felt, I could always find a way to overcome it and not be destroyed. In my wildest dreams, I never thought I could fall so far.

However, in the course of talking with my doctor, I realized that not only had I dealt with alcoholism on both sides of my family, I myself had experienced many of the events that could contribute to the onset of post natal depression. In the past five years, I had been divorced, gotten remarried, suffered a miscarriage, and gone through numerous rounds of fertility treatments. Someone who had been like a brother to me had killed himself, my father had died three weeks before my daughter was born, we had moved into a new apartment, and Rowan was born after a long and traumatic labor and delivery. To top it off, we had no baby nurse, we were inexperienced parents, my daughter had to wear a harness, my husband had to return to work in a different city two weeks after the birth, and I was inflated like a Macy's Thanksgiving Day Parade balloon. I was a textbook case!

I was still befuddled by the thought that I hadn't seen it coming. Could I have avoided any of it? I had never been sufficiently warned about the possibility of this type of depression. My doctor in New York had asked me once, early on, if I thought I might be a candidate for post natal depression, but I said, "Of course not." I had never fallen prey to any form of depression, and if the process of IVF hadn't sent me over the edge, then I thought nothing would. It didn't occur to me that it could have to do with a biochemical imbalance. The question I heard was "Do you get depressed often, and will you be unable to handle becoming a mother?" My response was so confident that the doctor had no reason to revisit the issue. An imbalance wasn't ever fully explained to me, and even if it had been, I probably still would have said I'd be fine. All I ever remember being told was that IVF drugs sometimes created PMS-like emotions, and that after giving birth, women sometimes went through a period called the "baby blues."

After I got pregnant, Chris once delicately asked me if I was at all worried that I'd get depressed after having the baby. I didn't even honor his inquiry with a serious response, because what would I possibly be depressed about? He had said that he knew I reacted strongly to emotional situations, and he wondered if the stress of the fertility treatments might take a toll. He obviously thought I might be susceptible, but I remained adamant that it would never happen. I never gave it another thought.

When my baby was only a week old, I knew something wasn't right because of the severity of my emotions, but I never dreamed they were due to post natal depression. And though my doctors had been helpful medically, it wasn't until I began reading other women's accounts in the material Sherie gave me that it became painfully clear. I could have been reading my own journal. Like me, these other women cried an inordinate amount and felt as if they had no connection to their infants. They felt guilty and mournful, and their minds were flooded with negative images of themselves dying or their babies being killed. These women had visions of suicide and terrible fears that they would never fall in love with or even want to hold their babies. A sense of disassociation and isolation pervaded each account. I was shocked that these stories related to me and that these women all sounded like sane, competent people. In almost every account, the people they told about their feelings responded that it was probably just the baby blues. Baby blues, my ass! That should be the name of a Saturday-morning cartoon. What we were all experiencing was full-fledged post natal depression.

I FINALLY HEARD the wake-up call and thought of my conversation with Kate Lear. She had looked at me with a deep knowledge of what I was experiencing and had reached out to help. As I read the article she had written for *Parents* magazine, I had so much more empathy for what she went through. And I had to admit to being a legitimate member of a depressed mommy society. Did this mean that I was crazy or that I was destined to be on the six o'clock news because of my inevitable actions? Of course not.

Evidently what we think of as post natal depression is a group of illnesses. There are the baby blues, quite common among new moms; here the mood change is mild and usually doesn't last longer than a few days to two weeks. Then there is post natal depression, which, according to the National Mental Health Association, afflicts 10 to 20 percent of women after giving birth. Basically, if this period of feeling depressed lasts longer than two weeks, or starts more than two weeks after giving birth, it is considered to be post natal depression rather than the blues. The most severe disorder is post natal psychosis. Women suffering from this condition may experience paranoia, delusions, or hallucinations and may lose touch with reality. It is rare and of course requires medical attention because these mothers are at risk of hurting themselves or their children.

In addition, there are a variety of post natal anxiety disorders that some women may experience, such as obsessive-compulsive disorder or panic disorder. While women with these conditions may be having scary thoughts—about hurting their babies, for example—they also recognize that their thoughts are illogical and therefore won't act on them. However, anytime a woman is having such thoughts, it's important that she speak to her doctor so she can get the help she needs. Also, it may be that severe post natal depression or post natal psychosis is actually the first sign of bipolar disorder—all the more reason to seek the guidance of a doctor.

I consider myself a well-informed, educated person. If this illness had taken me by surprise, I reasoned, I probably wasn't alone. Were other women enduring this in silence, either because they were unaware of what it was they were going through, or because they were too afraid to divulge their feelings? Maybe, like me, they just didn't believe it could happen to them. The more I learned about this illness, the more I wanted to find out what other people knew about it or had experienced. At first I spoke to acquaintances from the dog park or yoga class. I wanted to get a response from those who were not in my immediate circle, and it was easier mentioning it to people I knew less well. Many women I spoke to responded with "Oh, no, I never felt anything that bad. I was just tired and hormonal." Guys often simply exclaimed that pregnancy and childbirth made women crazy.

Later I talked to people I knew better. I got some shocked and contradictory responses. Some women looked at me with an expression of disdain; others tried to laugh it off or change the subject. Many said, "Oh, that's a phase you go through. It's just the baby blues!" It struck me as ironic that such a cute-sounding name would be used to describe such a sad time. If this had been an illness that affected men, I wonder if it would have been given a more serious, clinical-sounding name.

More than anything, I was curious. It hadn't occurred to me to feel bad about telling my story, but I started feeling like I was one of the few women who had experienced it and that it was not something one admitted to going through. I had been ashamed about not feeling a connection to my daughter, but I thought if I could get past the shame and be open about it, I might find solace. I didn't realize I would be so outwardly judged. I thought that if I talked about it, I would feel like I wasn't alone. I wanted to find the community of people who said, "Oh yeah, I felt the same way. Mine was bad, too, but don't worry, many mothers feel that way. It really will pass."

The problem was that I wasn't met with this response; instead, the opposite occurred. Most people couldn't believe I could have experienced anything so negative, because they know me as an eternal optimist. They would reply, "But you look great, and nothing ever gets the best of you. You seem bonded with your daughter, and you always have her strapped to you." It is hard to respond to a comment like this, and I felt like an idiot saying, "But I needed her strapped to me or I might have run away. Seriously. I was really the lowest I've ever been." The consensus seemed to be, "How could *you* be depressed, you have it all and are so lucky to have a baby." I started to feel like an even more horrible mother and that maybe there really was something wrong with me. Was I the only one who felt like this and was talking about it? This, quite honestly, angered me.

I couldn't believe people were being truthful. My mother has always said, "Don't take no for an answer." This was her way of teaching me to be a survivor, and it stuck with me. I decided to try again. I began by talking to people who did not have children of their own but knew people who did. Maybe they would be more open to discussing the issue. What I discovered was that every one of them had either a close friend or a relative who had gone through an experience similar to, or even more extreme than, mine. Was this the large white elephant sitting in the middle of the room that no one was supposed to talk about? I was persistent and decided to seek out more mothers. The more I shared my story and inquired about theirs, or about the experiences of those close to them, the more people slowly opened up. Soon, because of how honest I was about my terrifying experience, people started saying things like "Oh, no, I had it real bad." Or "Believe me, I know, my aunt was hospitalized." One person told me, "It got so bad, a friend of mine was actually standing on the window ledge of their apartment while her baby was in the next room." I was shocked by how many people had been as deeply affected as I was. Misery does love company. What I heard were variations of the following:

"I kept waiting for my baby's real mother to arrive."

"I thought, It's okay if my baby dies, because this is a bad world to grow up in."

"My friend couldn't walk by the microwave without feeling the incredible urge to put the baby in it."

"I couldn't even look at my baby for the longest time."

"I couldn't leave my bed for months."

"I didn't like my baby at all."

"I couldn't be left alone with my own baby."

"My husband had to remove all the sharp objects from my house."

"I cried incessantly."

"I didn't talk for a month and wouldn't leave my house."

"I couldn't stand the sound of my baby's cry."

"I wanted to run away and never return."

"I wanted to die."

"My family thought I might need to be institutionalized."

"My sister had to take my baby to her house until I was better."

"I didn't feel attached to my baby at all."

The more I talked to people, the clearer it became that not getting treatment of some kind was dangerous but that, with help, post natal depression would pass. Because people seemed to recover, I realized that maybe (as with the pain during childbirth) they wanted to forget it had ever happened. They tried to sweep it under the nursery rug or put it in the Diaper Genie and never face it again. Although people used different methods to help them get past the dark time, the most effective aid seemed to come in the form of a pill. This made me feel better about taking the medicine. In addition, many went to therapy.

It was comforting to know that those people who had experienced post natal depression but who had reached out for help not only came through it, they did so with healthy bonded relationships with their children. I was incredibly encouraged by this thought and was relieved to know that my relationship to Rowan was not going to suffer. A huge burden had been lifted by this revelation. I was pretty sure that my marriage would not suffer, either, but I knew that I would have to pay close attention to any pain I may have caused Chris and try to ameliorate it. The toll my depression had already taken, although not irreparable, had caused some real hurt. I would need to continue trying to be sensitive and aware. It was also becoming obvious that in order for me to fully recover from this depression and to remain cognizant of those close to me, I would have to do more than just swallow a pill. Because so much had transpired over the past few years, I now needed to address healing emotionally. It was time to start talking about my feelings with a professional.

CHAPTER 6

ARE YOU MY MOTHER?

I SPOKE WITH A DOCTOR who worked with women who had trouble getting pregnant for different reasons; he said that because the mind/body connection is so strong, he believed it was important for me to work with a therapist as well as take medication. He referred me to a therapist who he felt would be especially helpful in my recovery. I didn't have qualms about undergoing this kind of treatment and was committed to it. I had gone to therapy before and had found it worthwhile. Plus, I have always thought that going to therapy shows strength rather than weakness in a person. Though it can be hard and uncomfortable and not exactly what I would categorize as fun, the long-term positive effects outweigh any short-term pain.

Over the next few months, Chris and I stayed in the same city and were beginning to establish a regular routine. Each weekday

Chris would go off to work, and Rowan and I would start our day. In the evenings we'd all eat dinner together at home and then take a walk. Many nights, after Rowan was asleep, Chris and I would watch a movie. The consistency was comforting.

And once a week I spoke to a therapist about everything I was feeling with regard to my life and being a mom. She was a relative stranger, yet I poured out my heart to her. It amazes me how much easier it can be to talk to someone you don't know. In the past, my discussions in therapy had been focused on work, specific people, or daily problems; this time I was concentrating on an even deeper level, and what I discovered was much more profound. Exploring the issues surrounding motherhood was revelatory and cathartic.

Given my past work schedule, I'd gone to therapy only sporadically and often on a short-term basis. This time I had the luxury of consistency, and I settled into a different pace. I had time to think, ask questions, and allow my psyche to mull over whatever issues came up. In past sessions, I'd been used to coming up with concise answers to my problems. Now, between having a baby and the upheaval that creates, and raising questions in therapy that don't have definitive solutions, I was being forced to let go of my need for neat resolutions. It was scary and unsettling, but because there were no obvious solutions to any of the issues raised, I had no recourse except to keep moving forward.

When I first walked into this therapist's office, I was offered tea and directed toward a couch. As I moved toward my seat in this room with walls covered with archetypal images, I noticed a shelf filled with figurines and wondered if I was going to be asked to play some psychological game. Appropriately, I couldn't stop looking at the small ivory Virgin Mary. I wondered: Where should I begin? In this peaceful place, my mind was flooded with thoughts such as: What kind of a mom will I be? Will it be different for me because I'm older? How did my own mom fit in? How will I raise a well-adjusted, happy, healthy, and well-behaved little girl? How will I handle my mistakes? What if Rowan doesn't like me? How will I deal with my inevitable anger toward her at times? Is it okay for me to go back to work? Is it too soon to start working again? How has my life changed the most? How has my history affected my emotional state? How has my relationship with my husband changed? To what extent was the depression also caused by suppressed feelings about the devastating deaths of my father and close friend? Will I ever feel happy again?

The list didn't end. Up until now, aside from myself, I had been responsible only for my dog, and she never talked back or said, "I hate you, Mom!" What was I going to do when my daughter pushed me away? How would I react when she sided with her dad?

One of the issues this therapist helped me examine initially was what it meant to bring a child into the world. I had put so much time, effort, and emotion into getting pregnant that I had not really considered how my life might change once I actually had a baby. I had been quoted once as saying that, in trying to get pregnant, I had learned the difference between wanting a baby and wanting to be a mother. Looking back, I realize I hadn't fully grasped what that meant. I had faced such hardship in trying to get pregnant that I thought my commitment to motherhood had become much deeper than simply wanting a cute baby to hold. Yet I don't think I was prepared for the mind-blowing difficulty that accompanies having a child and the magnitude of what it means to have created a life. Imagining the three of us taking a stroll or all snuggling in bed together was a far cry from the reality of an infant screaming at three A.M. with a 104-degree fever. When I claimed I wanted to be someone's mother, I didn't factor in the devastating fatigue, the loss of personal freedom, and the overwhelming fear that are part of being a parent, not to mention the heartache. Chris and I were *responsible* for this new human being we had created. We were competent people, yet this was a much weightier responsibility than any associated with a pet, a job, or even a mate. There was no walking away from this one — a person's existence rested entirely in our hands. I had never thought of it in these profound terms.

In therapy I also talked about the rite of passage that occurs when one becomes a mother. I recalled being wheeled into the operating room to have Rowan; I felt uncomfortable kissing or needing my "mommy" and thought that maybe the torch does get passed on to the next generation in certain moments. I would always be my mom's little girl and would still desire to be mothered at times, but my loyalty shifted once I had a child of my own. From that point on, my child would come first. This made me sad and yet made me feel more grown up and empowered. I remember the first time I rode my bike without the training wheels on. We were on Seventy-third Street in Manhattan, and my mom ran alongside of me, holding the seat for a while. After a few seconds, I looked over and realized she had let go and was receding into the distance. At that point I almost lost my balance, but I righted the wheels and made it to the end of the block. Maybe it's a bit of a juvenile analogy, but it almost felt like once again the training wheels had come off and I was riding solo and away from

Mom. It was simultaneously frightening and thrilling. It had become time for me to enter a new phase of my life. This was a profound realization, one that took some time to digest.

FOR THE LONGEST time, I had been inextricably bound to my mom. Although I had spent time with my father's larger and more conventional family, the majority of my days had been spent alone with my more bohemian mother. It was a unique household to be brought up in, and I developed an intense connection with her. We barely shared each other with anyone else, and it was often us against the world. I trusted her completely and had faith in her ability to do anything. Even though I always went to conventional schools, my mom and I spent the rest of the time on movie sets, taking unique vacations, and in environments that differed a great deal from the ones the rest of my friends encountered. Because her approach was much more fun and carefree, my friends dubbed her "the cool mom."

My mother's word had been my gospel; I even thought she could make it rain. When I was about four, I got a raincoat and rain hat as a gift. I insisted on wearing them, even though the forecast was for a sunny day. My mom explained the weather to me, and I responded by saying, "That's okay, you'll make it rain, Mommy." Well, as fate would have it, by the time we got to the end of the block, it actually started to pour. I looked up at her and said, "You see!"

In a sense, I had always assumed that I was an extension of my mother. Then a 7½-pound little person made me reexamine a relationship that I had regarded in a certain way for over thirty years. I could gather strength from the fact that the existence of Rowan

Francis Henchy helped me to separate from my own mother. I am not talking about living in a physically separate environment, and I don't discount the individuality I feel with regard to my husband and my marriage. I am talking about discovering an independence in my head and in my heart as a result of becoming a mom.

Rowan also helped me to appreciate everything my mother has done for me. This woman has taught me a great deal, but I still needed to figure out what teachings I wanted to pass on to my daughter and what I wanted to leave behind. This task is required of all daughters who are also mothers. It's important for me to remember that I am not my mother, and I can define my relationship with my child the way I best see fit. My mother instilled in me good manners and a level of respect for others that, to this day, I believe is irreplaceable. She showed me the fundamental differences between right and wrong and what it means to be a decent human being. She nurtured in me the abilities to laugh, to love deeply, and to celebrate life. I am thankful for all of this and hope that I can instill the same values in Rowan.

Conversely, there are many things my mother did that I would choose to avoid in the development of my relationship with Rowan. My mom's fierce Mama Bear attitude allowed me to let my guard down and be protected from many of the pitfalls of Hollywood, but because we were so ensconced in each other's lives, I also let her carry many of my other burdens. For years I remained very naive, and even though I appeared to be mature beyond my years, I surrendered constantly to my extremely protective mother. There is a stereotype about how tough the business is, that it is full of sharks and people who either sell their own souls or try to hock yours. There's a reason such stereotypes exist. Because my mom tried to shelter me from engaging with these types of people or even being privy to their actions, I grew up a bit stunted in this respect and never developed my own protective armor. When I see how my business operates today and how people's feelings are disregarded, I am shocked.

Though my mom did everything she could to shield me from the business dealings, she never considered my looks as something to be protected, like an athlete's body. She was never too prohibitive when it came to playing, and I often had scraped knees and bruises from doing so. She tried to keep my life as "normal" as possible. I never went to a professional children's school, and I never missed more than the occasional day from class. My friends were mostly nonactors. As a result, my moviemaking was considered more like a summer-camp activity than a profession. While I was "playing" in my professional life and bringing friends with me on location, I wasn't witnessing the behind-the-scenes dealings. My mom, acting as manager, saw it all and fought for what she thought was best. I remained oblivious when people were negotiating deals or when my mom thought I was working too many hours on a set and chose to contest it. In our professional lives, she became the bad cop; I was the one who was never difficult, while she got the horrible reputation.

My mother has never been one to respect the establishment or play by the rules, and while she was fighting the system, I was the perfect, obedient, and well-liked little actress. Once, when I was working on my first big movie, *Pretty Baby*, my feet got severely infected because of the period shoes I had to wear. I complained to my mom, who wouldn't let me go back to work until the production company got me cleaner ones. As a result of keeping me from the set, she held up the entire production, and it cost them a lot of money; meanwhile, I went to a friend's house and swam in her pool. My mom did things like this all the time. I remained unaware of the havoc she often created while trying to protect me.

A relationship like this can serve as a real and complete comfort for a young child, but in certain respects it made me more vulnerable. It wasn't just in business that her strong personality rendered me less confident. In many areas, I never learned how to fight for myself or how to learn from my mistakes, because I had few opportunities to even make a mistake. For me, it's important to nurture my own child's individuality and strength. It's natural to want to protect your child, and I cringe at the thought of Rowan ever being compromised in any way, but I do want my little girl to develop a more solid sense of autonomy and self-confidence than I did growing up. I don't want her to be crippled by my desire to buffer her from the bad in the world. I had relied so heavily on my own mother to make everything right that I never learned how to do so on my own or for myself.

So often my mother's judgments—whether about a person, a boyfriend, religion, morals, even fashion—were so strong that they caused me to question my own views. When I was a kid, it was so intense that I even mimicked her tastes in food. If she didn't like something, I, too, found it unpalatable. Because I put such blind faith in my mother and in her choices for me, I didn't pay attention to the importance of cultivating my own beliefs and opinions. As a result, it became hard for me to listen to or know my own voice, and I often deferred to her view instead of discovering or expanding on my own.

It took me a while and a great deal of painful trial and error to emotionally free myself from my mother and to have faith in my own convictions. I learned this only at an older age; no doubt I would have been more personally empowered if I had developed this sense of self earlier. I would have liked to have had more self-confidence in who I was and in my ability to stand up for myself earlier. In addition, I believe that because I was equally tentative with regard to my professional abilities, my talent as well as my personal ambitions suffered. I got so accustomed to looking to my mother or to a director for approval that I never fully nurtured my individual creativity. If they said something was good, then that was good enough for me. I had experienced a taste of autonomy at college by exercising my mind, but it was limited to my studies. It was not until much later that I began to form my own ideas and speak out based on my creative instincts. Motherhood, and the increasing confidence it afforded me, furthered this growth.

After I had Rowan, my inner voice became much more audible. It was a revelation to me that just because my opinions were different from my mother's (and other people's), it did not mean they were wrong. When it came to raising my own child, it was as if I got to start all over again, and this time, I would follow my own instincts. This did not happen overnight; initially I had difficulty even finding my instincts because of the depression, but eventually my own solid beliefs and opinions surfaced. Of course, I have a husband with whom I share the responsibility of instituting these beliefs, but my mother's voice is no longer the loudest one in my head. I do not feel compelled to ascribe to her beliefs or to seek her approval for mine. I cannot say what contributed to this transformation, but it felt inherent in motherhood. I also can't honestly say that from the day of Rowan's birth, I never again needed my mother's approval in other areas of my life. It seems like a primal instinct to want your mother's endorsement, but it was liberating not to need it.

It was also an amazing moment when I recognized that Rowan was not my mother's daughter. My techniques in teaching her and my child-rearing philosophy could differ from my mother's, and I felt no need to justify them. I could understand how she raised me and acknowledge the difficulties she faced without having to model my approach on hers. In addition, I had lost the desire to force my mother to agree that my way was correct. I didn't have to fight with her on every little thing. Over the years, I had turned communication with my mother into a competition and had constantly tried to prove I was right. This mission seemed to dissipate when my own daughter arrived. Suddenly my mother could have her views, and I could have mine, and nobody had to win. I had become "Teflon Mom," and my blood pressure no longer rose every time my mom would start a sentence with "Don't you think it would be better if . . ." Instead I would respond with "Actually, Mom, I do not, but thank you for the idea." I even lost the sarcastic tone I often chose to use when trying to prove a point.

I remember making the decision to "Ferberize" Rowan so as to get her to sleep through the night. This is a system where you put the baby down to sleep, and while you comfort at intervals, you don't pick her up and you don't go into the room until a certain amount of time has passed. My mom was visiting on the second night of this effort. I had to sit in front of the door so she wouldn't go in and pick Rowan up. I laughed, because I was reminded of the *Mad About You* episode in which they Ferberize their baby. It was done in real time, and during much of the episode, the main characters were sitting on the floor outside of the baby's room, resisting the urge to go in. It was horrible hearing my baby cry, and I had an overwhelming urge to rush in and pick her up, but my real concern was my mother. Chris was in complete agreement that we needed to get Rowan on a schedule, and thankfully, she never cried for more than fifteen minutes. But my mom was up in arms. It was one of the first truly heated disagreements that my mother and I had about rearing my daughter. During our discussion, my mother informed me that I never cried as a baby. I told her I would alert the media and Ripley's Believe It or Not! that I was, in fact, the only child in history not to have cried a single tear!

I know my mother would have laid down her life for me if necessary. Now I was beginning to wonder what I owed my mother for her commitment to me. In my need to separate from her more fully, what, if any, was the debt I was meant to pay? Do I repay it by being as good a mother as I can be? And how should I include my own mother in this next phase of my life?

In my therapy sessions, I also pondered the level of my connection to Rowan. My mom bordered on the obsessive in her commitment to me, and I became her whole life. I was in a different position with my own child, yet that model was the only one I knew. I hoped for an intrinsic bond between the two of us. However, even though I was committed to Rowan, I needed to figure out where I would be creating my own boundaries. I came up with no specific conclusions for all these issues, but I began to fully recognize the existence of my feelings and how having a child had altered the way I viewed my relationship with my own mother and with my whole world.

Because I am sharing the parenting responsibility equally with Chris, I hope that Rowan will grow up with a more balanced life than I did. I also don't want my daughter to be badly affected by my looks or fame. Another therapist once said to me that she thought having a daughter would be more difficult for me than having a son. Her reasoning was that being the daughter of a woman who was often celebrated because of the way she looked would create extra pressure for a young girl just coming into her own. When I was a little girl, when we took the family Christmas photo at my father's house, he would single me out from all the other kids and say, "Brookie, don't pose!" All I was doing was smiling for a family picture and I was made to feel different from my siblings. His discomfort with my professional life, and my looks being the focus of so much attention, caused him to make a normal situation uneasy. I happened to be a model, but that didn't mean I was modeling twenty-four hours a day. I didn't like being singled out. The truth is that to a certain extent, all children are compared to their parents in some way, but my looks should not carry with them any extra burden for Rowan. Plus, I would hope that Chris and I are creating the kind of environment in which attributes other than physical appearance will be nurtured and respected.

Before Rowan was born, Chris and I talked about what kind of parents we wanted to be and the kind of environment we wanted to provide for our family. That conversation continues. We discuss being a real presence in our child's life. We are both adamant about being the ones to raise our child rather than delegating the responsibility to a succession of nannies. We want Rowan's world to include variety and excitement but not at the risk of compromising a feeling of security. We want to be the kind of parents who take our child everywhere and expose her to travel and many different environments. We agree that consistency and rituals are important. We believe in manners and morals and honesty. We want Rowan to feel safe, free, and happy, and that also means nurturing whatever she has an interest in. Faith is something we want to uphold but in a way that is less dogmatic than the way we were exposed to it growing up. Communication is one of the most desired qualities we want in our home. In past relationships, both Chris and I have admittedly experienced the negative effects of not communicating. We both want to communicate more fully with each other and have it serve as an example for our daughter. It's exciting to dream about how we'll raise our family, and it's even more exhilarating to realize that most of these dreams can come true.

I CONTINUED GOING to therapy and taking my medicine. As time passed, our lives became more settled, and I was beginning to feel more peaceful. I was focusing on my family and on getting healthier and happier. Because of his work schedule, Chris still wasn't able to get home before Rowan went to bed, so he had to wake up almost as early as she did in order to spend some time with her. They had a sweet little ritual. After I got up with her, changed her, and eased her into the new day, Chris would feed her and either take her to the dog park or they would go outside and watch the birds. Rowan would squeal at the sight of Dad, and after the handoff, I could take a shower and down some much needed strong coffee. Rowan loved the regularity of her routine, and we all seemed to be getting the hang of our new life. She began consistently sleeping through the nights and taking regular naps. The roots of family life were taking hold.

Emotionally I was beginning to feel more and more what I had thought a mother would feel (as opposed to a depressed mommy). Rowan's voice became much more than a bark or a cry. She'd laugh when tickled, and I'd feel a surge of pure joy in my stomach. Whenever Darla came to sniff her or sneak a kiss, Rowan would let out a high-pitched scream. I started saying, "Where's Darla?" and she'd look around. I'd heard of the simplest things being exciting to a mom, and I now knew exactly what that meant.

Rather than feeling like it was an intrusion, I started to enjoy planning my day around Rowan's schedule. I was amazed by how fast a day could pass in doing things that, to my pre-baby self, would have seemed unproductive. These activities centered on the life of a four-month-old and focused on food, education, and recreation. Every day I made sure Rowan was having "tummy time," when I would put her on her stomach so that she could lift her head and strengthen her neck. There was also "alone time," when she was in her crib watching a mobile or listening to music. I had read many of the baby books about the stages of development and tried to include their suggested activities without becoming completely obsessive. (This time I actually remembered what I'd read!) I also had to face the fact that Rowan was a human being and would no doubt surprise us by doing things that were not discussed in the books. I read to her each day, and she loved seeing colors and hearing the different tones of my voice. I made sure she had time to play, got plenty of fresh air, and had her naps. Add in time for breast-feeding and baths, and the days flew by. I was exhausted but found solace in the fact that my mood was better and that I was in a rather manageable routine. Chris often felt like he was missing out on all of the activities during the week, but he got caught up on the weekends.

We never spoke to Rowan using a baby voice, but all bets were off at bath time. I made up various voices to correspond with the different washcloth hand puppets that we used. Most of the voices were a combination of Julia Child and Cookie Monster, but I did whatever it took to make my "little bug" smile. And boy, did she smile! Rowan began to laugh even louder and kick her tiny feet in the tub. She looked so sweet, with the few hairs that she had standing up on her perfectly round head. I'd gently pour water from a cup onto the top of her head to get her used to the feeling, and she would squeal and look at me with anticipation of the next pour.

Another thing that contributed to my more positive mood was the fact that I could start exercising again. The recovery from my C-section and my injured uterus had so delayed the possibility of exercising that I was beginning to feel uncomfortable and weak. I have always exercised, and not being able to do so was very difficult for me. The adrenaline and endorphins associated with exercise have always been something I have needed and enjoyed. Because I had been able to be active during my pregnancy, it was a shock to my system to stop exercising so drastically after giving birth. I am sure that the lack of physical activity was not helpful in my recovery from post natal depression, either.

Finally I had gotten the okay from my doctor and began going on long hikes in the hills with Rowan strapped to my chest. She no longer had to be in her harness, so she fit even better in the

BabyBjörn or my New Native sling. She loved being close to me, and I took pleasure in knowing she was happy and I was getting my body moving again. Once outside, she usually fell asleep within twenty minutes, sweet and rosy-cheeked. I loved to stare at her while she slept. Sometimes, while hiking, I'd stop under a tree and watch her steadily breathing with her tiny mouth slightly open. I vowed to remember each of the good feelings I was experiencing.

The bigger Rowan got, the better a workout it was for me. I began to get stronger by the day. Usually it was just the two of us, but sometimes a friend would join us. While my friend walked next to us, I would put Rowan in the stroller and do the hills so my arms could get stronger. Every once in a while I'd meet up with another mother and her baby, and we would drive to a different location to hike. I was rarely without my little girl and was beginning to develop a tangible connection to her. I took videos and pictures of her and quickly filled up three albums. She was growing by the minute, and I created a flip-book of her image taken in the same spot each day. I had done the same thing of my stomach when I was pregnant. When you peeled the pages of the book back and slowly released them, you could see my stomach getting bigger and bigger. It was harder to document a squirming baby, but the daily changes were amazing.

I did have some nightmares about the black cloud descending again. I was far from fully recovered, and sometimes I dreamed that I had lost my daughter or that, no matter how hard I tried, I couldn't complete a task that involved her care. After these dreams, I'd wake up scared and unsettled for a good portion of the day. I felt like I had severe jet lag or some kind of hangover. Chris reminded me that the dreams did not mean I was spiraling out of control again but that I should try to keep track of my moods just in case. Sometimes Rowan seemed to react differently if I was in one of these moods. She'd fuss or stiffen her body and cry in response to my voice. This would signal me to try to lighten up for her. Her own mood could turn on a dime with the right distraction. I tried to forget the dreams and not fall prey to my fears.

I spoke to my doctor about what portion of these feelings was caused by the post natal depression and what was due to common parental worries. She said that I would probably always be worried about something, and that the moment I became a parent, I gave up the luxury of sleeping through the night. From now on it would be "fireman's sleep," meaning that even the smallest of noises would wake me up; a part of me would always be on the alert and ready to care for my infant. Any number of normal maternal issues could be causing the fears or the dreams, but as long as they didn't escalate further or start to strongly interfere with my day, then I was probably experiencing the general angst that comes with being a mom. The feelings would most likely balance out, and the dreams would probably stop. The doctor added that she could try me on another medicine or give me a stronger dose of the one I was already on. I really did not want to experiment with different drugs at this point, so the dosage remained the same. I was also worried about what would happen when I stopped taking the medicine. Yet even with some of these interrupting down periods, my overall situation seemed less dire. I had felt so much worse during those first few weeks of Rowan's life than I did now. The bad thoughts and deep, unsettling fears did not, in any way, pervade my day as they used to. I could wait these episodes out.

It helped that we had a sociable little girl. I took her to baby showers, parties, and restaurants. I even went with her on a playdate with four other mothers I didn't know. It was at the home of a photographer friend of someone I had met at the dog park. We all went to her house for lunch, and then she took a group picture of the babies all lined up on a fluffy rug. Rowan was the youngest and smallest baby there, but everyone remarked on how sweet she was and how mature she seemed. She was funny and animated and loved being with these people and the other babies. I felt like I was making a new friend in Rowan. I actually liked her more each time we ventured out together.

Although it was fun going out, we also loved being at home together. I'm better at setting a table than making a meal, but Chris and I work well as a team, and prepared delicious food on the weekends. We really enjoyed the quality time we were spending with our daughter and were establishing new traditions. Among my favorites were omelets and whole-wheat pancakes on Sunday mornings and chicken with green chilies on video night.

I could tell my husband was glad that I was getting help and that I was obviously feeling better. His whole demeanor was lighter, and his sense of humor was back in full swing. It had lapsed for a bit during the rougher times, but he had even returned to making fun of me for things like my malapropisms and the fact that when I drive, I sit too close to the steering wheel. These jokes used to be a regular occurrence, but it had been a while since he felt the freedom or the desire to make them. Chris was relieved that the waters were currently smooth. Sometimes he'd wait and watch my reactions to Rowan's crying or to any of the daily frustrations I had. It was as if he wanted to make sure none of it would put me over the edge, like it might have in the recent past. He would quietly sigh in relief when I didn't become upset.

Even though it seemed to me that Chris was holding his breath, hoping my mood wouldn't change, it was clear that our marriage was going to survive and had, in fact, become even stronger. We had great talks over dinner, and I began celebrating our daughter and our life together the way I had hoped to. We'd stare at her and marvel at how remarkable she was. Raising her was the most inspired endeavor we had ever embarked on. We were finally having fun being parents. The dark dreams began occurring less often, and I started feeling more like a regular mother who had rational concerns about her little girl.

Now that my thoughts were less bleak, I found myself mulling over when and how I would return to work. We had settled into a healthy routine, and even though I wanted to work again, I felt torn. I believe that in order to be a whole person and feel a sense of pride in who I am, I need to be able to both work and be a full-time mom, which to me means being there as the primary caregiver but carving out a schedule that allows me to have a career as well.

Being a mother is one of the most difficult and rewarding jobs a person can have, and I have never underestimated its all-consuming nature. I admire those who can be stay-at-home parents, but I know that if I did that, I would eventually become unhappy, and so would my daughter. I would never just hand her off to someone else to raise, nor would I give up my career, in part because I want to instill in her the feeling of empowerment you get from having work that you love. Did I have to apologize for wanting to do both?

I am still amazed by how strong societal expectations are. I have heard women sound apologetic when they say, "I'm just a stay-at-home mom." Conversely, if you work outside the home, you feel guilty. Society seems to celebrate those who have their children one day and then return to work the next. In other cultures, women are allowed to rest and nurture their newborns before returning to their other work. With the help of many others, they are allowed to recover and then resume their lives. In our society, we are supposed to either quit completely or act as if nothing has changed. I realized early on that I would probably have to alter the intensity of my work if I wanted to be an effective mother, but what I didn't realize was how hard it would be to find the right balance. In the past, I would revel in the unpredictable nature of moviemaking and the spontaneous and widespread travel required. It excited me to be able to live in a different city or country for as long as it took to complete a project. I didn't mind temporarily leaving behind the life I had at home. My world would revolve around the movie and the crew and all that came with it. Chris's writing allowed him to be mobile, and he would often stay with me on location for long periods of time. I still wanted to work, but the more acclimated I became to motherhood and home, the less I wanted to leave the life we'd created. Though I wanted the creative outlet, I wasn't sure how I'd react to the nomadic life I had lived in the past.

I got a glimpse of what my working life could be like when I did the commercial shoot for Bright Beginnings, which was shot in Los Angeles. This was the job that I had signed on to do when Rowan was very small—the meeting where I cried. For the first time since having my little girl, I felt emotionally and physically prepared to step in front of the camera. I had lost some of the baby weight and looked more rested than I had in a while. Because Rowan was only five months old, I brought her to the set with me and got a friend of Gemma's, who lived in L.A., to stay with Rowan in the trailer. Having my daughter with me was a luxury that I didn't take for granted. She was able to be on the actual set when we weren't shooting with sound, and everyone fell in love with her. The shoot lasted only two days, and the people involved were extremely nice. They had wanted to use Rowan in the commercial, but I had nixed that idea a long time ago. As the people cooed over her, I could tell they still hoped to use her in the ads but would never ask. I was still breast-feeding, and everyone on the shoot was sensitive to my daughter's schedule. Even though it was for a formula commercial, they made every effort to plan the shots around her feeding and give her a private room in which to "dine." The wardrobe was simple and comfortable and the makeup and hair were natural. In each TV spot, I was a young mom having fun with her daughter but doing so in a less than perfect way. The scripts were funny, and it felt good to get back to work with a comedic part.

We shot two commercials. In one, I was trying to make different animal sounds to get the baby to laugh. I got to act like a complete idiot, and the kid just stared blankly. When I got to the elephant sound, I could not do it without sounding obscene. Everybody got more hysterical the harder I tried. In the other spot, the baby watched me poorly lip-synch a song from the 1980s. I danced around the kitchen and then tried to make up for looking like a fool by switching to a classical tune. It felt wonderful being funny, and even though people couldn't make noise while we were rolling, they burst out laughing as soon as the director yelled "Cut!" During one of my breaks, I called Chris to tell him that it was going very well and that even though it was tiring, I was glad I took the job.

It was a small taste of what it would be like to combine my personal and professional lives. I did feel waves of guilt whenever Rowan wasn't in my arms, but it all seemed rather manageable. It felt good to be doing what I loved and not have to be completely away from my daughter. I was exhausted, but this was what I had hoped to be able to experience as a working mother, and I was encouraged. I began feeling more empathy for those moms who had to leave their infants once they returned to their jobs. If I navigated my work properly, I might be able to be a mom and a professional without too much angst. I would not be forced to choose and therefore could enjoy them both.

CHAPTER 7

MOTHER
LOAD

THE TWO-DAY SHOOT FOR Bright Beginnings had been a good preparation for my next job. It helped me to realize the possibility of being a working mom; having my baby with me made all the difference in the world. When my next job offer arrived, I wasn't as concerned that I would feel compromised in one area or the other.

I got a call to do an as yet untitled project with Scott Glenn; I've been a fan of his ever since he swallowed that worm in *Urban Cowboy*. It was a four-hour miniseries for cable in which Scott was to play a killer and I would be his attorney. I had never played a lawyer before, and I welcomed the opportunity to work with Scott. Plus, I could again bring the baby and a nanny on location in Sacramento. I never would have left the baby for any reason and would have turned down the job if I couldn't bring her with me. I was getting more and more attached as time went on, and I didn't want to do anything to alter this feeling.

My therapist and I both felt confident that I could take the job and check in with her periodically by phone. There would always be things to discuss in therapy, but thanks to our work over the last few months, she had helped me get to a good place, and I was physically and emotionally strong enough to leave the confines of my current routine at home. These phone sessions would be fit into the filming schedule and would help me to stay on track and serve as a sort of safety net should I start to feel depressed again.

Rowan was almost six months old and was still breast-feeding, so this production company also had to be comfortable with the fact that I would need to take scheduled breaks for her feedings. In addition, they had to be informed that I had no plans to get any thinner for the part. I have never been told I needed to lose weight for work, but I was still carrying some extra pounds from the pregnancy and would not be able to lose them until I stopped breast-feeding. Luckily, no one had a problem with the "healthier" Brooke, and I took the part.

I was excited by the prospect of acting again in a movie and looked forward to focusing on my professional duties rather than on the color of Rowan's poop. Don't get me wrong; her bodily functions had been the highlight of my past few months, but it would be a welcome change to be consumed by such tasks as learning my lines, concentrating on my acting, and not being late for my call times. It would be only a two-month shoot, and because it was such a short flight from Los Angeles to Sacramento, we could come home on my days off. Chris was still working pretty hard but would visit on weekends. The best part about the whole plan was that Gemma was able to come with us, and her family was able to care for her son. I knew how intense movie shoots were and how long the workdays could be. I probably wouldn't have felt comfortable with anyone else looking after the baby. Gemma would keep Rowan on a schedule and not let making a movie interrupt it. In addition, she would guard Rowan with her life and make sure that my daughter and I weren't away from each other except when the camera was rolling. Gemma came out first to Los Angeles to help us get ready, and we packed up more gear than I have ever taken to a movie set before.

When on location, I usually try to make my hotel room as comfortable as possible and bring with me whatever creature comforts I can. I have been known to turn even the simplest of motel rooms into a home away from home. This time, instead of doing so with candles and stereo equipment, I was lugging things like a bottle sterilizer and a Pack 'n Play. What a sight we were, running through the terminal (because, of course, we were late—something I never used to be): a six-foot-tall woman holding an infant in one hand and a breast pump in the other, and a petite Filipino woman rolling an ExerSaucer in front of her and holding a music-playing Pooh bear on her hip. We got looks of both sympathy and amazement. It was clear that the people who recognized me couldn't believe how unglamorous I looked. Some of the less polite ones even commented on this. Very few people tried to help and instead said things like "Not as easy as people think, huh?" or "Don't you just love traveling with little ones?" I chose to ignore most of the comments because, quite frankly, my responses would have been bitchy, and I didn't want to say anything I'd regret. Some people just wanted to get a glimpse of baby Rowan, but it was hard to be polite and have a chat, since we were trying to catch a plane. We finally got through the gate and collapsed in exhaustion the minute we sat in our seats.

Once in Sacramento, we got settled into the hotel. I began working almost immediately, and for the first time on a film, I didn't need a wake-up call. The baby got up early enough for me to feed her and play with her a bit, and then either I brought her to the trailer with me or Gemma brought her after her morning nap. I was amazed at how quickly we all got into a routine and how adaptable Rowan was. When the shooting schedule switched to nights and we filmed from the early afternoon until early in the morning, I got to spend even more time with my little bug. If my call wasn't until later in the afternoon and Rowan was napping, I got to work out in the ho-tel gym. I missed my husband, but we spoke several times a day, and we both were relieved that I was managing at least part of the work/family balance that I had envisioned. Rowan's bedtimes and mealtimes didn't vary from their usual times, and she visibly enjoyed the new experiences and different people. Her eyes got wide every time she met a new person or we took her to a different area of town. She especially loved the river and kicked her little feet so fast when she saw the boats with their flags flying.

Chris enjoyed visiting because we all got to explore a new city to-gether. When I was on the set, he got to have uninterrupted time with the baby without having to worry about his own work responsibilities. The transition for all of us seemed surprisingly easy, and since we didn't have any major upsets in Rowan's day-to-day life, doing the movie appeared to have been a good idea.

Usually on TV or movie sets, the assistant directors yell over the walkie-talkie, "Quiet, please, we are rolling, no walking, no talking, and no cell phones." On our set, however, because Rowan was there with me, they started adding, "No crying on the set, and no spitting up on the wardrobe, please, we are rolling!" It was so sweet to see how the crew welcomed Rowan. Often someone would make her a toy out of gaffer's tape and clothespins or do something to make her laugh. Even the older, more cynical grips and electricians would soften in her presence.

The movie was shot at a fast pace; at first this was fine, but it didn't take long for me to feel completely spent. I went to sleep exhausted and woke up feeling no more rested than I had been before going to bed. Instead of being energized throughout the day, I couldn't wait for the next break and until the wrap was called. I got paler and paler, and the circles under my eyes became more pronounced with each passing day. The breast-feeding was depleting me of any energy I had, and even though I looked forward to hearing the director say that it was "cookie time" for Rowan so I could return to my trailer and feed her, I started to wish the filming would end. It became evident that the schedule was harder on me than I had thought it would be. I had anticipated that with Gemma's help, I would be able to adapt to the rigors of filming a movie as easily as I had in the past. Except now I was a mother. After a few weeks, I began missing Rowan's bedtime on a regular basis and would get back to the hotel long after she had fallen asleep. Then, more often than not, I'd have to leave too early in the morning to wake her up. I started to resent not having the freedom to drop what I was doing to play with her or to not care if my clothes got soiled with milk. The idealized version of being a working mom and the reality were proving to be quite different; this was exhausting! Like working moms everywhere, I had the feeling that I was being pulled in too many different directions.

It was different for my husband. When it came to child rearing, we had both adopted the roles more traditionally assumed by our respective genders. Of course Chris and I had talked about how we saw our individual roles within our family and home, but this was the first time I had seen it all in action. We were a dual-career household, but there were times when only one of us had a job. I had been the one primarily at home with the baby and did not know when or where my next job would be. Chris had gone back to work without feeling much conflict, except for missing our daughter during the day. It seemed normal that he quickly went back to work while I was left at home to care for our child. When I say "normal," I mean that we never questioned it when Chris returned to work as if nothing had changed in his life. On the other hand, since I was considered the primary caregiver, I had to find a way to navigate my work around caring for our child. I wasn't mad about this as much as I was fascinated by the fact that even though we considered ourselves a modern couple, Chris and I weren't far from the conventional parents of a generation or two ago. He did do a generous share of the daily baby care, but it was never questioned that his chief role was to work and support his family while I was Mom. I appeared to be the only one questioning and analyzing the whole dynamic. It was interesting that

Chris wasn't at all conflicted about trying to balance the two areas of his life, whereas I was quite torn. Though he missed Rowan, it was never an option for him not to return to work. I, too, instinctively believed that I was the mother and therefore should be the more hands-on caretaker, but I also never imagined myself not working again.

As the movie shoot progressed, I continued to feel pulled in two directions. My head was in the work, but my heart was back at the hotel room or in the trailer with my daughter. There were specific things I enjoyed doing with her that I found comforting and that I was missing out on while I was working. For example, when Rowan would see the BabyBjörn, she'd make this funny "ooh, ooh" sound because it meant we were going for a walk, but I couldn't go on many of these walks during the filming. During bath time, she'd slap the water with open hands and emit a deep belly laugh when I'd scream at getting wet, but now I'd get home after bath time. And the look in her sleepy eyes while I nursed her in the evenings filled me with such peace that I looked forward to it each night, but often I'd have to settle for pumping so Gemma could give her the bottle. I found myself asking Gemma, "Did she do her little wiggle?" or "Did she hold her bottle by herself?" I knew these were all little things, but I was upset about missing them. It was easier when Chris was visiting because our family felt more complete. Even though she was in very good hands with Gemma, I was so sad every time I had to return to the set.

My life on the set was different, too. Instead of playing a joke on a crew member or games with the cast in between setups, I couldn't wait to get back to my trailer. I knew I needed to forge ahead with my work, but I also wanted to fully enjoy my little girl. Of course,

Rowan remained unfazed by my dilemma and went about her day like there was no problem. My work didn't seem to suffer, but I was beginning to feel overtaxed.

Rather than maintaining my initial enthusiasm about the movie, I started to complain a bit to my husband that I was getting worn out. Soon my calls home were fewer and shorter, and Chris heard the tension in my voice. He became concerned that I had taken on more than I should have and that it was too soon to juggle so much. He had supported my decision to go back to work and had faith that I could do it, but he wanted to make sure I was taking care of myself. In our phone calls, he would ask if I was eating enough and getting sufficient rest. Because Chris wasn't seeing me every day, he had a tougher time recognizing my actual mood, so I promised that I would tell him if I started to feel overwhelmed or emotionally delicate again.

I wasn't as concerned with my food intake or my lack of sleep as I was with the fact that I was having trouble remembering my lines and enunciating them clearly. It dawned on me that it might be because of the medicine I was taking. I hadn't noticed it before because I hadn't needed to memorize lines or perform in front of many people. Maybe I had been a bit forgetful at times, but I was a new mom and had chalked it up once again to fatigue. In this environment, it was much more obvious, and it quickly became a problem. The dry mouth that I was experiencing was manageable, but not being able to remember whole pages of dialogue or speak without sounding like I had a mouthful of peanut butter was not ideal for an actress. Normally I never have trouble with my lines. Now I was lucky if I remembered the name of the character I was playing. At first I thought I could work through it, but it started to become embarrassing. The crew tried to make me feel better by joking that I was drunk and that "cookie time" was really Mama's "vodka time."

Because of what had happened the last time I went off the medicine, I was afraid to stop taking it. I called my doctor and asked if switching to another medicine might help. She knew me and my medical history so well that prescribing the next medication would not be difficult for her. It might be trial and error for a few weeks, but she had seen good results with several different drugs. I was skeptical of trial and error because I was more familiar with the "error" part of that phrase. Again the doctor had to promise me that the new drug would be safe for breast-feeding, that it was not addictive, and that I could go off it eventually. I followed her direction, and the next drug I tried made me way too sleepy. When I took it in the morning, all I wanted to do was nap, and when I tried taking it before going to bed, I had trouble waking up in the morning. This was not ideal for someone trying to prove she could do it all! My issue with this drug became evident in just a few days, so the doctor switched me to another medication. Luckily, we found that Wellbutrin worked perfectly for me. There were no bad side effects, and within a week I noticed a significant difference. Soon I sounded less like Foster Brooks and was able to memorize my lines without becoming frustrated.

All those months when I felt so low, I had been obsessing about going back to work. Now I was feeling that work was much harder than I'd anticipated, and I needed to figure out how to deal with these competing interests. I was becoming quite tempted by a desire not to work. Unfortunately, I was only halfway through with the film, and I had to do my best to finish the job in a way that made me proud. I would need to try even harder to balance both areas of my life. First I decided that I wasn't going to accept less from myself in either area, so I reanalyzed my schedule and decided which things I might be able to cut out in order to be able to focus more on my baby. I knew that many women have to juggle their work and their families, and I was already in the privileged position of being able to have my child with me every day. I gave up my time in the gym and decided to nap with Rowan if I wasn't yet on the set. I stopped returning phone calls during downtimes if Rowan was awake, and instead read her a book. I asked for my lunch to be put in a to-go container and brought to my trailer so I didn't have to waste time waiting in the lunch line. This made me feel more in control, and I was able to get even more serious about my work and my time with my daughter.

I negotiated with the production company so I could spend as much extra time as possible with Rowan. Sometimes that meant my call times were switched, and other times it meant asking if my scenes could be moved around so I could put the baby to bed. I even waived my call times so I could be with her more. Actors are supposed to get a certain amount of hours in between one day's wrap time and the next morning's call time. I said they could call me in earlier if it meant that I could see Rowan in time to put her to bed. It wasn't always easy, and there was an entire crew the company had to think about, but they tried hard to be sensitive to my requests. It required a lot of organization and time management.

Even though I was getting this project under control, I would still have to figure out in the long run how I could balance a career with being a mother. In my profession, there is a tremendous amount of pressure and competition, and you must be willing to withstand it all and practically be available 24/7. Except with a sitcom, whose schedule is set, if a job comes up, you take it and go wherever you are asked. This makes it difficult to establish any kind of routine or to make or keep plans.

The desire to achieve a certain stature and make sure you take advantage of every opportunity seems to be what fuels many to stay in the game. It can be quite ugly, but if you believe in your work, you are willing to endure it and forge ahead. I knew I wanted the work and could handle all that it entailed. But what I hadn't realized was that I wasn't willing to sacrifice time spent with my little girl. I was beginning to question whether I wanted to do this kind of work for fourteen hours a day, especially at such an early stage in my daughter's life.

This project was almost over, but I began to realize that I didn't want to spend Rowan's formative years working so hard that I missed out on the miracle I had as a daughter. How would I make my life work given the profession I was in? It does afford you a certain freedom, because you can take your kids with you, but what happens when they start school? And although I had my daughter with me on this job, I had to admit that I missed not spending whole days with her.

Chris never complained about the fact that he was left alone during this time and had to do most of the traveling to be with his family. Although he was such a good sport about our temporary stay in Sacramento, I knew he must feel like he, too, was missing out on the baby during the week. To make him feel less lonely, I did the unthinkable: I started putting Rowan on the phone to "speak" to her father. This is a huge confession, because I used to hate it when my friends would make me talk to their infants. I'd cringe the moment I'd hear "Here, speak to Auntie Brooke!" I'd have to stop my conversation and stay on the line to listen to heavy breathing and sounds of spit. Much to my chagrin, I became a full-fledged member of this community of prompting mothers and slobbering infants. I got such joy from calling Chris at work and saying, "Okay, on the count of three, start talking to the baby." He loved hearing her breathe and had to deal with the strange looks he'd get from his writing staff as he spoke in exaggerated tones to someone who didn't even have teeth. And I didn't do it just to Chris. I couldn't help myself. I'd put Rowan on the phone so my mom could hear her laugh or a friend could listen to her voice. It got so bad that whenever the phone rang or I said hello, Rowan would hold anything she had in her hands up to her ear and look up expectantly. Of course, I considered this brilliant behavior and would lunge for the video camera.

I kept up the rather frenetic pace of making the film and being Mommy, and the new medicine worked very well. Each night I passed out the moment I hit the pillow. When we were finished with the project, I felt like I had basically kept it all together in a way that satisfied me. Luckily, my relationship with my husband was strong enough to weather this period of time. I would never want to put our marriage on the back burner, but for now Chris helped me to feel that I could put more of my energy into balancing motherhood and a career and that as a couple we would not suffer.

After the movie ended, it was almost Thanksgiving, so we flew back to Los Angeles to drop off some of our extra things and then went to New York City as fast as we could. Gemma made the trip to

Los Angeles with us and then went on to the Big Apple to be with her son. I have always loved spending Thanksgiving in New York, and to this day it remains my favorite holiday. We usually spend the day with close friends and therefore don't have to deal with any family pressures. It's different from the holidays like Christmas and Easter, when people disperse to their individual families. With Thanksgiving, you're freer to create your own traditions. I love the feeling of a full table, lots of food, and a room buzzing with conversation between people from different walks of life. For me, it's all about enjoying the festivities and the food in a relaxed and joyous atmosphere.

This year I wanted to have plans because it was our first Thanksgiving with a child, and it felt like, finally, I was part of a complete family. I wanted some time to pause and acknowledge how blessed we were to have one another and to have survived the hardships of the last few months. I also wanted to start creating our own family traditions, though I was too exhausted to host a dinner at our apartment. In addition, because we had planned to have Rowan's christening the day after Thanksgiving, there was already a lot to organize. Since this was the only time that was convenient for everyone, it had been scheduled months before. We'd definitely see our fair share of blood relatives that day, so it was even more important for me to spend some time alone with Chris and the baby before the family arrived.

This particular trip to New York was also the first time that we were returning to the place where the most frightening and dramatic part of my post natal depression had occurred. I was a bit afraid of going back to the apartment, because I was worried about revisiting the site of such unhappiness. On the way from the airport,

I felt a pit in my stomach. I was scared of the possibility that, in my return to where it had all happened, the same feelings might resurface. We arrived in the evening, but because my mind was in a much healthier place than it had been, I felt like I was actually walking into our new home for the first time. The smell of the apartment even seemed different, and there was a warmth to it I hadn't sensed before. What a contrast it was! Where I had once felt only fear and a terrible sense of isolation, now I was secure in my love for my daughter and in my abilities as a mother.

We had been invited to have Thanksgiving dinner with Anna Strasberg at her apartment on Central Park West and decided it would be an easy and comfortable way to celebrate. Anna, who had been married to Lee Strasberg, still teaches and conducts workshops for actors. I had been lucky enough to be directed by her a few years back, in one of a series of plays in New York. After we worked together, she sort of took me under her wing. I often call her before starting a project and talk to her about the character I am about to play. Meals at her home always include interesting and talented people and wonderful food. There are pictures of amazing actors everywhere, and she has fascinating stories about all of them. Whenever I go to her house, I feel as if I'm a member of an eclectic, artistic extended family. The apartment is on a high floor, which means that it is eye level with the balloons in the Thanksgiving Day parade. I had never seen Rowan's face more animated than when she watched the likes of Snoopy and Barney float by, filling the window. She squealed, pointed, and made her "ooohhh, ooohhh" sound during the whole parade.

After we enjoyed a wonderful holiday with new and old friends,

Chris and I decided we'd walk back to the East Side instead of taking a cab. Rowan was in festive dress, but we had bundled her up. We had on hats and scarves, and the wind gave us a rosy flush. We decided to stop and have a drink at a hotel on the way home. I stuck with Perrier, and Chris had champagne. As we sat and looked out the window at the fast-walking people and the passing yellow taxis, I felt the wave of contentment I had always thought I'd experience in being with my husband and daughter. Chris and I toasted the one thing we were most thankful for. We looked into each other's eyes and we both said, "Rowan." She gave us an innocent stare, and at that moment, I knew everything was going to be all right.

Rowan's christening was held in Old St. Patrick's, the oldest church in New York City. We invited only a small number of family and friends. Gemma had spent the holiday with her family but came to the house to help us get ready for the event. She brought Rowan a Tweety Bird cake that said, "We love Sweetie Pie." We decided to serve it at the celebration that followed the service. The cake was a perfect addition because Rowan was looking more and more like Tweety Bird every day. Her blue eyes were huge, she still had no hair, and her forehead was quite pronounced. We laughed at the likeness.

The ceremony was incredibly intimate and very touching. Breaking with tradition, everyone was allowed to come toward the altar to closely witness the rituals performed in a baptism. I dressed Rowan in a long white linen and cotton dress that had not one ruffle on it. It had taken me months before she was even born to find one so simple. I can't stand glitz. Every christening dress I had ever seen was covered in ruffles and frills, and I had been determined to find a simple one. My mom had given Rowan an antique bonnet and a beautiful silk cape to go over the dress. Once Rowan was dressed, she looked like a Victorian baby princess.

The ceremony was just the right length, and people commented on how moving it was. Chris and I remained rather relaxed, except for being a bit distracted by all of our family members being in the same room, and hoping everyone was getting along. I had forgotten how important and pressured christenings could be. They are treated like mini-marriages, and besides the fact that they do represent a type of spiritual union with the church, the ceremony itself is held at an altar and feels a lot like a wedding. Chris and I got teary and looked at each other and our daughter with such affection that I felt warm all over. The priest spoke about choices people make and the power of commitment and the love we share with one another. He said that, as in choosing to marry a particular person or deciding to have a child, the choice to baptize is incredibly important and involves responsibility. A baptism is a rebirth and means that a commitment is being made. He highlighted how ritual is an important part of whatever faith a person has, and he said that a baptism is not only a new beginning but also an opportunity for all of us to be reminded of what is individually important in our lives. He was a Catholic priest, but what he was saying pertained to those of any faith. His words centered on the ideas of love, commitment, and responsibility.

I looked at my friend John Kimble, Rowan's godfather, who had flown in from Los Angeles the night before. His eyes said how thankful he was that we were all healthy and had come to honor this little girl as the blessing that she was. The last time John had been with us in New York City, I was at an extremely low point, and he was quite scared for me. It was obvious from his expression now that he was relieved to put it all in the past. He stared at me and the baby, and his eyes were glistening.

While we were still in the hospital, we had asked Chris's sister, Michele, to be Rowan's godmother. I had barely uttered the question before she burst into tears. She kept thanking us and crying. Now, as we all stood at the altar, with Rowan in Michele's arms, we could practically see the love and pride like a halo around them.

After the service was over, we all headed to an old bar called P. J. Clarke's. The weather wasn't great, but we put Rowan in an old-fashioned pram that we had gotten as a gift and walked to meet the rest of the party there. We chose to go to P.J.'s in honor of my father, who, with my mom, used to bring me there when I was an infant. In fact, I was brought to the same spot after my own christening and was placed right on top of the bar. We put Rowan there and held up our beers to toast both Francis Alexander Shields and Rowan Francis Henchy. The fertility doctor I occasionally saw in New York and the doctor who delivered Rowan even stopped by to give toasts. We ate the best burgers in town and celebrated until extremely late. Rowan had fallen asleep in my arms, and because she was obviously exhausted from the past few days, she hardly stirred at all, even when we made the transfer into her crib at about two A.M.

Because Chris had two more weeks of work before the Christmas/ New Year hiatus, we were going to be in the city only one more day before returning to Los Angeles. And what an extraordinary day it turned out to be! My mom, who lives in New Jersey, had been coming into the city every day to see the baby. She usually returned home after Rowan's bedtime. She knew that Chris and I had hardly spent any time alone together since Rowan was born, so she offered to babysit while we had a date the Saturday after Thanksgiving. We decided to go to dinner in the neighborhood before Rowan's bedtime. I gave her a bath and passed her over to my mother to feed her a bottle of my pumped milk. Well, all hell broke loose! Rowan would not take the bottle from my mother and screamed like she was in pain. I heard the noise as I got to the elevator and came rushing back into the apartment. I took Rowan in my arms, and she quieted down right away. I knew my mom felt bad, but it meant the world to me that I was the one my daughter wanted.

I guess that whatever insecurities I'd had about her loving me had made me feel as if I wouldn't be special to her. In the first few months after she was born, I'd had such a hard time feeling anything for her. My therapist helped me to understand it was possible that what I also had feared was that my daughter would reject me and never really love or want me. In reaction to this, I had retreated and put up a wall around myself. The distance I had inadvertently created also could have been some sort of reaction to safeguard myself from getting hurt. I couldn't explain this insecurity, but it seems like a rather common defense mechanism. I was as afraid I wouldn't become attached to my daughter as I was that she wouldn't become attached to me. Now I saw how unnecessary it had been to place such pressure on myself and on my infant.

As I soothed my baby girl by holding her close to my chest, I felt a deep connection to her. Up until that moment, I had felt my love for her grow, and I was able to enjoy who she was, but I hadn't received the same kind of love or validation in return. I rocked her for a while and thought that this must be what people talked about when they said, "There's nothing like it." It is so strange to want validation from a baby, but I realized that had been a part of what I was experiencing all that time. The moment Rowan was in my arms and content, I knew I mattered to her. The fact that I meant more to her than my mother was monumental. It is embarrassing to admit, but it is no secret that I had—and still have, to a certain extent—an incredibly complex relationship with my mother. As I have said, separating from her has always been an issue for me, so when I felt my daughter's desire to be in my arms rather than my mother's, it was profound. Because I'd grown up so strongly deferring to my mother, I subconsciously assumed my own daughter would do the same. When it came to the love of a child, I even believed my mom would somehow enchant my infant, just as I had been enchanted as a child.

My therapist had a field day with this stuff, though it wasn't a new concept for me to bring up in therapy. The post natal depression seemed to magnify the insecurity I felt in relation to my mom and to Rowan. I had worked hard to find the places where I was merely projecting old beliefs onto the current situation.

Holding Rowan, I felt special and needed. I realized there was an undeniable bond between my little girl and me. It couldn't be usurped by anything or anyone. This was unique and it was ours. Rowan finished her bottle and went down without a fight. My mom said, "She loves you so much, sweetheart." I could tell my mom felt bad that the baby had cried in her arms, so I explained empathetically that it was just because she was more used to me. I knew my mother had wanted to be able to comfort the baby herself, and I assured her that soon Rowan would fall asleep in her arms as well. I was telling my mother that it was going to be all right. Talk about a rite of passage!

Chris and I left and, over dinner, discussed how having babies changed the way we viewed our own parents. Chris talked about how, before Rowan's birth, he had been a husband and a son, and those had been his primary roles. Now he was a father, and that took precedence over his relationship to his own parents and created a different dynamic with his wife. As the previous scene with Rowan so clearly demonstrated, my own loyalties had shifted as well. We continued to discuss how differently we regarded our lives now that we were parents. It was such a relaxing and lovely night. We stayed out way too late, and the morning came much too soon.

As nature would have it, my personal bliss from the night before vanished. When Rowan woke up, I brought her into bed with us until it was time for packing and her feeding. After some time spent being cozy together, I tried to take Rowan out of her dad's arms and into her bedroom rocking chair to feed her. She pushed me away with straight arms and screamed. All of a sudden Rowan had decided that now she was daddy's girl. She could have gone to her daddy the night before, but it was obviously my turn then. I had thought in the morning she would still want only her mama and was hurt that I had to pry her away from her dad. I guessed I was going to have to face the fact that a child will probably always switch affections back and forth between parents. Eventually I became the heroine once again when I presented her with what only a full-breasted mother could. I took solace in this and in the previous evening's event and held them close to my heart. I carried this warm feeling with me all the way back to Los Angeles.

CHAPTER 8

AND THEN
THERE WERE
THREE

THIS TIME WHEN WE WENT back to Los Angeles, I was in much better shape. On the plane, the focus was on keeping Rowan happy, not Mommy! The flight attendants took turns holding her, and she loved seeing the overhead lights go on and off. I was looking forward to going back to the West Coast, especially because I wanted to have a check-in session with my therapist. Despite my good intentions, I hadn't been able to talk to her while doing the movie. Needless to say, there was some catching up to do.

This time I spent the hour with my therapist talking about the fact that working while having a baby was not the relief I had thought it would be. I admitted to being very conflicted about my priorities. It was interesting how different these sessions were from the earlier ones. I caught up as much as I could and joked about returning after my next therapy hiatus with another entirely different point of view. I was surprised by the fact that talking about Rowan only made me want to run home and see her. I had brought her to the last session before our trip, and the therapist was completely enamored.

Because we were in Los Angeles only a little while before returning to New York for Christmas and New Year's, it seemed like no sooner had we arrived and settled in than it was time to begin packing up for the next holiday on our real home turf. No matter where I am, I return to New York City for the major holidays. Luckily, because Chris is also from New York, he, too, likes to return to the Big Apple for Thanksgiving, Christmas, and New Year's.

This trip was going to be important because it was Baby's First Christmas. Baby's first anything is always fun, especially with a first child, but there is something extra special about the initial Christmas. I have the funniest pictures that my mom took on my first Christmas, and I'd always planned to document my child's first one as well.

Though I love the idea of Christmas, I've always been a little disappointed by it. The buildup was always so great, and the anticipation so strong, that it never turned out as I had hoped. My friends would all tell me about their family rituals and the things they couldn't wait to do during the holiday, and it seemed like so much fun. My Christmas was always split between my parents: I would spend Christmas Day with my mother, and on the twenty-sixth, I'd head off to my dad's to celebrate with his family. My mom was never close to her family, so it was usually just the two of us; it was always so quiet. And by the time I got to my dad's, the festivities were already over. I was never able to experience the traditions usually associated with the holiday. I hated being the only one opening a present and always brought everyone more than one gift so the attention wasn't only on me and what I was unwrapping. My dad's family did include me warmly, but it was always a bit uncomfortable. I saw holiday sights and had fun with my mom, but when it came down to the actual day of Christmas, I used to get a bit sad that my mom and I didn't have a big family to be with. My parents individually were loving and generous, but I secretly wished for one big family who ate good food together and used the time to forget their disagreements and be thankful. It sounds like a Hallmark card, I know, but it's clear that I have sometimes chosen to live in a fantasy world, creating perfect family moments in my head.

I know a lot of people get depressed around the holidays, and maybe I am no different. While my post natal was at its height, I had become even more fixated on this notion of the perfect family and the perfect mother/child bond. Therefore, I became even more adamant about changing my own holiday history.

I kept my promise, even if I did go a bit overboard in decorating the apartment. I put twinkle lights everywhere and lit so many candles that at one point the smoke alarm went off. The place screamed of the holidays. Chris and I had planned a fun family Christmas week that was chock-full of activities. We would take our picture with Santa, see the windows at Saks and Barneys, watch the lighting of the tree at Rockefeller Center, have a live tree of our own that we would decorate together, and cook a great meal on Christmas Eve and on Christmas Day (well, Chris would do the cooking, but I would help create the holiday-themed meal).

First stop, Macy's! When I was a kid, my mother used to take me there every year. The Santas always looked a bit stoned, but they were very jolly. I used to get so excited to sit on Santa's knee, get a candy cane, and have my picture taken. There was just one Santa, in the center of the store, and you waited in a medium-length line to have your visit with the bearded St. Nick. You'd watch the other kids sit with him and whisper in his ear and hope that what they'd asked for wasn't the same thing you wanted. I'd be all dressed up and giddy as we inched up to the roped-off Santa chair. The anticipation was more than I could bear. I had a collection of the many consecutive years of photos and one year had put them all in a book as a Mother's Day present for my mom. I hadn't been back to Macy's in almost a decade, not since I had performed a song from *Grease* in front of the store for the Macy's Thanksgiving Day Parade.

Now we dressed Rowan up in a little red velvet dress that had a white boa trim on the hem and cuffs, and we got to the store as it was opening. It's a good thing, too, because the line was already beginning to form. How things had changed since I was a kid! Now a trip to visit Santa had become a huge production. Not only was there an enormous line that went practically throughout the whole store, but there was more than one Santa. I didn't realize this at first, but as we made our way through the line and were surrounded by moving elves, toy trains, and huge candy-cane makers, it dawned on us that the families were all being guided through different hallways that led into different closed doors. It was like a big holly-and-pine-wreath-covered maze that had different Santas sitting at different finishing spots. Chris and I joked with the salespeople, who were dressed in green velvet dresses or lederhosen with pointy elf shoes. Chris whispered, "Come on, give us the inside scoop on your best Santa!" They swore that there was only one Santa and he couldn't wait to meet little Rowan (wink, wink). The trip through Santa's workshop took almost an hour and, I have to admit, I was the one who played with every interactive toy they had. Chris kept telling me I was holding up the line.

Once we got through our door, we were in a room covered with tree branches and fake snow. Rowan got a surprised expression, and she stared at Santa without making a sound. I couldn't tell if she was frightened to death or mesmerized by it all, but as she sat on Santa's knee, she stared straight out with her mouth wide open. (Click!) We then decided to take a family photo, so Chris and I got on either side of our shiny-faced Santa, who looked like he was made out of wax. We put Rowan in the middle and tried not to laugh. (Click!) We then got a number, and it was entered into a computer. A second door then opened, and we filed into another line to choose what photo package we wanted and receive our photos. This line was also long, and I was beginning to be recognized. This is always an uncomfortable situation, and the worst part is that all it takes is for one person to single me out and then it's much easier for everyone else to follow. It gets a bit crazy at times, but I can usually get through it fairly quickly and without too much stress. Having Rowan with me made it feel much more invasive, and I didn't want so many strangers getting in her face. The poor thing first had to deal with wax-museum Santa, and now she had parents pointing at her and yelling to their kids that "Brooke Shields is here with her baby!"

Being recognizable is hard enough, but being with a baby gives people even more of a reason to talk to you. It's similar to when you're pregnant and strangers feel as if this gives them a reason to touch your body. Rowan still had her mouth open, but she didn't appear disturbed by any of it. We got up to the register and saw the photos. Rowan looked like cute little Cindy Lou Who from Whoville, and Chris and I looked like overweight, pale prison escapees. I had never seen a worse photo of me or of Chris. He joked that if either of us had seen this photo before we met, we never would have said yes to a date. It was funny until we realized that the elf staff had made multiple copies of this photo in order to get autographs. Putting on my best holiday smile, I had no choice but to sign "Merry Christmas" on the mass-produced horrible photos. Of course, we bought key chains and photos of all sizes of Rowan with Santa, which we distributed to our family.

Next came the buying of the tree. We bundled up the baby, took the dog, and walked over to the west side to pick out the perfect first Christmas tree for our baby. I took pictures of Chris carrying her in the BabyBjörn with the tree on his shoulder. It was such a beautiful image that I cried.

On Christmas Eve, Chris and I drank rich hot chocolate and decorated the tree. I gave the baby a box filled with unbreakable ornaments, and she threw them everywhere. We then made a big deal of turning on the lights all at once to surprise her. Rowan loved the lights but moved on quickly to the boxes that the lights had been stored in. She tired herself out throwing the boxes in the air after filling them with anything she could find. It was time for a bath, a story, and her evening milk. I put her in candy-cane-striped footed pj's and played soft Christmas music. As I nursed her in the rocking chair and sang "Silent Night," I quietly thanked Santa for granting me my wish.

As usual, Rowan went to sleep in her crib without a problem.

I went out to sit with Chris and got another huge mug of hot chocolate. (I believe that no matter what form it is in, you can never have
too much chocolate, especially dark chocolate.) We sat together and
talked about my earlier difficulties and how far we had come. I recalled how desperately I had wanted to feel connected to Rowan
and how I had longed for this blissful family experience. And now
here we sat, snug in our apartment on a cold Christmas Eve with
our baby girl tucked safely in her crib, enjoying the warmth of each
other's company. It was such a contrast to the emotional heaviness
that had existed just after Rowan was born. Chris and I had to take
stock of the differences, and even though I wasn't totally "cured," it
was a glorious feeling to know we were together as a loving family.

On Christmas morning, Rowan had the same reaction to her
presents that she'd had to the lights and the ornaments. She threw
away the wooden walking dog and put the box over her head. Antic-
ipating that this might happen, I had also wrapped up some empty
boxes for her to open. I think she enjoyed them much more than
any of the other gifts. We opened up our presents, and then Chris
made Christmas-tree-shaped pancakes and my mom came by for a
late breakfast. (Chris's family was coming into town the next day.)
We dressed Rowan up in a beautiful Christmas dress and little Mary
Janes and walked to church for mass. It was one of my first Christ-
mases when I didn't want to be anywhere else.

I know families are never perfect, and I am learning to let go of
wishing they were. I also know that we are given what we are given,
and it's up to us to decide how well we accept this. I hoped to create
tradition for my family because I missed it growing up. My daughter
may grow to hate it, but like my parents, I can only do my best.

The rest of our Christmas season was spent visiting friends and enjoying the cold weather. We had planned on going to Palm Beach to visit the mausoleum where my father's ashes were, but I was still not up to the task. I avoided dealing with my father's death and often pretended that he was still in Florida. I had briefly touched upon it in therapy, but as it turned out, more of what I talked about centered on feelings about my daughter and the post natal. I realize it was unhealthy to avoid dealing with my feelings about my dad sooner, but I had no excuse other than I just couldn't. My stepmother, Didi, who rarely comes to New York, had not yet met Rowan. Although I wanted her to meet her beautiful step-grandchild it would be a while before I'd be ready to be back in my dad's home. I continued to send Didi updated photos of the baby, and she sent Rowan some beautiful gifts, including a sterling-silver baby cup that had belonged to my father and was engraved with his name.

I remained incapable of facing the reality of his death, and to be even more honest, I'm still struggling with it. I find I miss him more and more as time goes by. Sometimes, out of the blue, I'll burst into tears. But I'm dealing with it in my own way. One thing at a time.

So we canceled our plans to spend New Year's in Florida and chose to stay in Manhattan. I have always felt that New Year's Eve is overrated and that people try too hard to have fun. This year, because we stayed in New York, Chris's parents extended their trip and baby-sat. Once more, I had to give the baby her milk. This time, however, we avoided all the tears. Chris and I had another date that included seeing a play and ringing in the New Year at one of our favorite restaurants. We toasted to our daughter and to my feeling better.

In Chris's toast, I sensed a slightly skeptical tone as he remarked on how much healthier I appeared to be. I could tell he wanted what he said to be true. I realized that he needed to be reassured that I was, in fact, okay. Again I promised to tell him if I started to feel low. I could tell he didn't fully trust me, and even though this made me feel bad, I knew I had to be compassionate toward him and sensitive to his feelings. If I happened to be having a down day, he would ask, "Are you having a slip?" I would try not to get defensive or be insulted and instead find credible ways to quell his fears. I made sure I reacted calmly to stressful situations and tried to look for humor in things. I was always searching for activities I could do with Rowan, in the hope that Chris would see me engaged with our daughter. I played more music around the house and took more of an interest in what was going on in Chris's work life. Depression is a very self-absorbing affliction, and when you are in it, it is so overwhelming that it's hard to think of anybody else.

My own fears of a slip did exist and were exacerbated by Chris's tentative attitude. I started trying to prove to him and to my close friends how much I loved our daughter and how happy I was with my life. I always dressed her in special outfits and included her in all of our plans. I made sure I was the one who put her to bed and got her out of her crib in the morning. I never made dinner plans that would interfere with putting her to sleep, and I preferred to invite people over so we wouldn't need a babysitter. I enjoyed all of this, but it got a little excessive. I began trying so hard to make it obvious that I was a good and attentive mother that it was becoming tiring. I had such guilt about having experienced a dark time with my daughter that I wanted to make up for it. It was as if I had committed some crime and needed to preface everything with "Look, everybody, look at how rehabilitated I am. I am even better than before!"

Even though I was enjoying my little girl, it felt forced. I remember saying things out of the blue like "I just love being a mom!" At times I even looked at my husband directly in the eye and said, "You know I love her, right?" In my attempt to demonstrate how much better I was, I would add facts about how one's hormones play a role in the illness and quote such statistics as "One out of ten women suffer from post natal depression" to show that it was much more common than one might think. I needed to prove to everyone that I really wasn't a bad mother and that I could be trusted. The truth was that I needed to trust myself first, and I wasn't fully at that point yet.

I was noticeably better, but it would still take time. What if the depression came back? What would happen when I went off the medicine? I felt unsure of my improved state of mind because it was so new. I had been consistently feeling better ever since I started the Wellbutrin, but how would I know when I was totally beyond the label POST NATAL DEPRESSION? Believing everything was going to stay positive was not going to happen immediately.

It had taken me a while and a great deal of help to come this far, and I'd have to be my least favorite thing: patient. I would have to accept that those beginning months had taken a certain toll on the people around me, and that gaining their trust again would not happen overnight. Just as people had to deal with the shock of seeing me in such an emotional state after Rowan was born, so, too, would they need time to adjust to my healthier frame of mind. One of the other things I had discussed with my therapist was my guilt for even having post natal depression. She said that it was pointless and that I needn't feel guilty or embarrassed about having suffered from it. She said it was understandable but unnecessary. Not only could I not go back in time, but I had been working hard at dealing with it. Slowly I broke my rather pathetic habit of telling practically everyone I met how much I loved my daughter and started understanding that my actions would speak for themselves.

It took time to decipher the difference between healthy, realistic fear and other emotions associated with being a parent, and those linked to post natal depression. Having a baby is difficult enough; even under ideal circumstances, it is an incredible adjustment. Once you have been given a diagnosis of post natal depression, it is hard to know whether what you're feeling is "normal." Every time I worried about something regarding Rowan's care or behavior, I wondered whether my thinking was colored by the depression I'd been fighting. Was I okay, or was this the start of another depressive episode?

I kept thinking about what I feared the most in raising my daughter and started to see that even more than mourning my old life and the freedoms that I thought it afforded, I was worried primarily about failing. I worried that I wouldn't know how to raise my daughter to be a kind, thoughtful, and polite person who had strength and confidence. I worried that one day she would hate me and would wind up in therapy, complaining about how her mother had messed her up. I was afraid that my child wouldn't think I was the best mom she could ever have and wouldn't love me deeply. It scared me that I needed so much from her. I continued to talk to my friends who were also parents, and when I recognized how common so many of my concerns were, I felt relieved. I felt sad at times, but so did most of the people I knew. It didn't mean that I was getting depressed again. Nobody knows what they're doing when they first have kids, and I wasn't going to fail, because it wasn't a test. As long as I tried, I would pass. There was more than one acceptable way to raise children.

I recently saw a play that a friend of mine was in, about child abduction. Watching it, I became almost physically ill. I felt such empathy for the mother. I used to be emotionally moved by things to which I had no connection, but this went to the depth of my soul in a way I never could have anticipated. After the play, my friend apologized for not warning me. She doesn't have kids and said she thought I could separate myself from the horror the piece portrayed. That experience exemplified yet another way parenthood transforms you. My husband can't watch shows about ills done to children and switches the channel if one comes on. For me, becoming a mom has brought to the surface a sensitivity the depth of which I never knew existed. It's hard to explain except to say that I feel more vulnerable and stripped of my personal defenses than ever before, and yet in some ways, I feel stronger. For me, becoming a mother also means that I feel happier than I could imagine and more sad than I thought possible. None of this indicates that I am crazy or in any way abnormal. Basically I am just more alive and present in my own life than I ever remember being.

THE NEW YEAR brought with it a great deal of promise. We felt as if we had been given a fresh start, and both Chris and I were excited to shake off the residue of the last year and begin anew. Chris had to return to Los Angeles to finish up his writing season on *I'm with HER*. I planned to take Rowan and go back with him until after Valentine's Day. Chris and I are part of a group of four couples who have developed the tradition of spending the evening of Valentine's Day together. That year it was our turn to host. I decorated the table with hearts galore and designed the food to be either red or Valentine's Day–related. I have a girlfriend who is a chef, and she helped out with the food. I had the added joy of dressing Rowan up first as a fairy to greet the guests and then in a beautiful red dress with a smocked front. Another couple had brought their little girl, and it was a fun playdate for everyone. We each made toasts, and our friends all mentioned how thankful they were that Rowan had arrived in the world safely and that her mom was adapting better and better each day. It felt good to be among friends and wanting to celebrate.

I sat at the head of our dining room table, opposite my husband and with Rowan on my lap. As Chris held his glass up to me and winked, I was struck by a feeling of melancholy. I remembered my dad winking at me whenever we made toasts at dinner. I was overcome with a variety of emotions, and my feelings of love for my dad and for Chris were overwhelming. For the longest time, the sentiments I had surrounding my dad were only of sadness and loss, but in that moment, I felt a rush of happiness and remembered how close I'd felt to him. It made me smile. Sitting there with my baby in my arms, I just knew my father would have adored her. Surely Rowan would have been the recipient of one of those same winks. It had to be enough to know that. I became too choked up to add to Chris's toast, and our friends soon were looking at me with concern.

I assured everyone at the table that what they were seeing were tears of joy, love, and thanks and that no one needed to worry. The jumble of feelings rushed in so fast that it took me a little while to fully relax. I sat back and just watched and listened for a bit. I felt surprisingly at peace. I let myself savor that emotion and soon joined in on the lively conversation. I hoped I wouldn't always have to be making disclaimers about my mental state, but for now it seemed only fair to do so.

After the toasts, Rowan went to sleep in her crib, and the other little girl fell asleep on our bed surrounded by big pillows. The dinner animatedly continued on. By the time we got to the heart-shaped cookies, Cupid cake, and red sugar cubes, I had been completely ridiculed. My only defense was that it would never be in my nature to do anything halfway. My friends would have to love me even with all my obsessive tendencies. One friend said, "I suppose we will all be taking home little heart-shaped boxes filled with red heart candy?" I looked at her with disdain and acted insulted. "I beg your pardon; do you think I would do such a dorky thing? They are heart-shaped mirrors and little combs to put in your purses!" My best friend added that we should never expect anything less from the woman who probably even had a cozy made for her answering machine. Everyone laughed at my expense, and it felt good to be back.

By the time the end of February rolled around, Rowan had decided she'd had enough of Mom's boobs. Thankfully she didn't reject my breasts, but she started drinking less, and soon I stopped producing as much milk. It was a surprisingly easy transition, and a sadder event for me than for her. Although I continued to try to pump, she weaned herself and wouldn't stay latched on as long. Soon she was completely on the formula, and I was going through it by the case. This was a big change for me, as we had spent so much time together nursing. I went through a bit of mourning because I really missed this kind of closeness, but I knew there'd be plenty of other activities to share. This taught me that just when you get into any kind of a routine with your baby, she changes and you have to adjust all over again. I realized that the unpredictability of parenting was probably never going to end. I laughed at how much we all try to beat the baby system by being prepared for everything, and how the one thing we aren't ready for becomes the one thing sure to happen.

Coincidentally, just as we all got comfortable in Los Angeles, it was time to return to New York City for an extended period of time. It was a work hiatus for Chris, and that meant a longer time off than for the holidays. I was looking forward to being able to stay for more than a week and to further enjoy my hometown with our daughter. As luck would have it, just after we settled into our East Coast life, I got a call for a job on *That '70s Show* as a very sexy recurring character. I'd play the mother of one of the young girls on the show who shacks up with the father of the other young girl. The guys on the show all have crushes on this character and fall all over themselves when she's around. I was told I would be playing the "MILF"(Mother I'd Like to F—). I had never played that type of character before, but the actors involved were all sexy themselves, and the thought of being the object of their affection was a real ego boost, especially after having had a baby and never thinking I'd get back any kind of sex appeal. The part was quite funny, and taking it would mean that I'd have to go to Los Angeles for a few days each month. Although this has always been the nature of the entertainment business, and I have always loved such spontaneity, I knew that with a child, it would not be as easy to keep moving around. But because I would really enjoy playing this role and I wouldn't have to be away for long, I took the part. It didn't seem worth it to bring Rowan on a long plane ride for the two days of the first episode, so I decided to go alone. I was no longer giving her breast milk, so Chris could handle the baby at night on his own. I could jet off to La-La Land for the taping.

The whole idea sounded slightly irresponsible, and because it would be the first time I had left her behind, I wasn't sure how any of us would react. It would be strange not being with Rowan after such a long time of practically being glued to each other, but I also secretly felt excited about having some time to myself. I thought I could see friends, go to a movie, take a yoga class, and most important, sleep in until I woke up. Even though I planned to fill the two days with a ridiculous amount of activities, not to mention the job I was going for, I felt like I would be playing hooky and wanted to fit in as much as possible. I brought books and magazines and looked forward to the five-plus-hour flight, during which I could actually watch the movie and have the meal. It didn't matter if the food was terrible; the point was that I would be waited on and not be on baby duty.

As usual, things didn't work out as planned. Not only did I become gripped with fear during takeoff, but once we were up in the air, I kept trying to call home. I was focused on the fact that I was leaving behind the two people I loved the most in the world, and I didn't want anything to happen to any of us. Feeling a little bit paranoid, I wondered if it was the post natal talking. I calmed myself down and kept busy until we landed. It helped that I had brought a travel photo album of Rowan that I showed to all of the flight attendants and anyone else who was interested. The pendulum kept swinging.

Once I got home from the airport, I called Stephanie, and we made our plans. I settled into the empty house and figured I would get my first good night's sleep. Unfortunately, I couldn't fall asleep for the longest time. I finally drifted off only to wake up a few hours later, at exactly the same time Rowan would be waking up. I was on her time clock, and my milk even came through a little. I couldn't believe that even though we were separated by thousands of miles, I was still physically and emotionally attached to her. What a far cry this was from the beginning of our journey together, when I would have given her away! Here I was with two full days of freedom, and all I could do was think and talk about her incessantly. I missed her terribly and wondered what she was doing each minute.

I called New York practically every hour, or at least when I knew Rowan wasn't sleeping. One time Chris exclaimed, "I am walking to the play group with two other mommies and babies, and I haven't had a shower or a real meal since you left. I used to think you were being dramatic when you said you couldn't even take a shower when taking care of this baby!" I laughed hard and was glad he had empathy for the plight of a mother. I think all dads should be left alone with their infants at least once. The level of respect they would gain for their partners after experiencing one-on-one baby time would be monumental. Each time I phoned, I asked Chris for a play-by-play of what Rowan was doing and made him put the phone to her ear so she could hear my voice.

The second day I was gone, Chris called and said, "You are not going to believe it, but Rowan crawled today!"

"What? I have been with her twenty-four-seven for nine months, and she crawls the day after I leave?" I couldn't believe it. I almost wished he hadn't told me and then acted surprised when she repeated this move in front of me.

Chris knew I'd be upset about missing it and quickly said, "Babe, she was looking for you!"

That was fast thinking on his part, and I pretended it was true. What's strange is that Chris is much more cautious than I am regarding Rowan's movements. I have always tried to give her more freedom to roll over or sit up and wanted her to feel comfortable and secure in her environment. It never occurred to me that I wouldn't be the first one to witness such a momentous achievement. Later my oh-so-funny husband called and said, "Oh my God, Brooke, Rowan walked upstairs and made me coffee this morning. You better get back here before she's doing long division." Ha ha. Hilarious.

I so missed my family and even though the job was fun and rewarding, I couldn't wait to see my little bug again. Chris was having such a good time taking care of Rowan and going out to eat with her. He didn't keep her completely on her schedule, but it was actually okay. This was a good lesson for me, because I was so focused on keeping her on a routine that I wasn't allowing for any spontaneity.

The vision I had of baby Rowan and her dad at a downtown restaurant, sharing an evening meal, was so sweet. It made me very happy. My trip ended up being a good thing for all of us. I was made to feel like one of the cast, and I adored doing a sitcom after such a long time. On the flight home, I was more relaxed and thankful for experiencing another example of how I might be able to juggle my work and family responsibilities. I also realized that, because all of my jobs are really different, I would probably have to keep figuring this out day by day and navigate one job at a time. Even though I'd been preoccupied by Rowan while I was away, I realized that this, too, was a normal condition of parenthood. I would probably never again feel whole or complete without my child, and I'd better get used to it.

The first thing I did when I got back to our apartment in New York was to kiss my husband; then I rushed off to take a bath with Rowan. It was just around bath time, and I knew she was excited to play in the water. I had planned my return trip so I could arrive in time to put her to bed. In the bath, we splashed and laughed and played with toys by putting them in and taking them out of a net basket. We made a mess, and there was water everywhere, but I didn't care. I felt so carefree, and I was giddy with laughter. Her little naked body felt so smooth against my own, and at one point she tiredly collapsed on my chest with an actual sigh. I held her close, and right after I sighed, she quickly popped up and wanted to play with her bath book again. I stared at her for quite some time as she opened and closed the thick waterproof pages, as if reading a classic. I wondered how much she knew about what I had gone through and how different I felt now. She was laughing and handing me puzzle pieces from the book and appeared no worse for the wear.

At that moment I knew I was older and wiser than she was. Strengthened by my current state of confidence, I was able to see that, earlier, when I believed my infant was all-knowing, I had been governed by insecurity. An infant is so unpolluted and unadulterated that there seems to be more room for knowledge as well as clarity. The truth was, however, that my years had earned me wisdom and experience that a newborn could not yet possess. The thought that had been in my head from the moment she was born was that she was somehow infinitely more aware and capable than I was. The purity of Rowan's soul and her quiet regard made me think that she was taking everything in and processing it through a complex computer. Honestly, her seemingly wise gaze at birth had scared me. Looking at her in that tub, splashing and making raspberries with her wet mouth, all I saw was a tiny baby girl who had a playful soul. We loved and needed each other. I was shaken out of my reverie when, as I reached over her head to add more warm water to the tub, she saw something she recognized—and chomped down on my nipple. She did it quickly and then looked up at me with an impish smile and crinkly little eyes. "Aahh," she added, tilting back her head. I responded with a tickle to her chubby tummy.

All clean and slightly wrinkled from the water, we wrapped up in robes and towels and sat in a rocking chair in her room. Rowan and I cuddled quietly in her little bedroom, and she calmly drank her bottle. I put my head back and realized that this feeling of complete peace and pure and absolute love that I was experiencing was what parents had been talking about all along. I was where I was meant to be, and I didn't want it to be any other way. I dozed off for maybe three minutes and felt more relaxed and content than I had in a long time. When I came to, Rowan's eyes were getting heavy, and she was done drinking. I eased her into her crib, gave her the cach*cach* (a little satin and flannel blanket with an elephant on one corner), and she went straight to sleep. That night I, too, slept like a baby.

CHAPTER 9

OUT CAME
THE SUN

AS I WRITE THIS, IT HAS been over a year since the dramatic
birth of my daughter and my struggle with post natal depression began and over three years since I took the initial steps toward having
a child. My particular journey into motherhood could not have
been further from what I had expected. From the day I walked into
my fertility doctor's office, I seemed to have entered an altered state
of being. Looking back, I am not quite sure who it was living my life.
I was going through all of the motions, but I never felt like I was in
my own skin. Had I stopped to calculate the odds of getting pregnant, I might never have had the strength to continue. All I could
see was the finish line. Finally I have returned to this world, and although I am different, I am also stronger and a great deal happier

than I had ever hoped to be. For the first time in a long while, I feel as if I am back in my body and fully engaged in my own life.

Going through post natal depression was the most frightening and devastating challenge I have faced to date. Having a miscarriage was in many ways overwhelming, but it wasn't mind-altering, and I had a reason to continue. Losing my friend David to suicide was shocking and changed my life forever, but I carry him with me wherever I go, as I do my father. I have felt deep sadness and loss, but I had never before faced such acute fear or had such a strong desire to die. Living through those long months after giving birth has given me a deeper appreciation of my daughter than I might have had if the experience had been easier. In addition, because the depression leveled me, I was forced to analyze myself more deeply than I would have ever done by choice.

In the past, I never had trouble doing something once I set my mind to it. So it didn't occur to me that I might not be able to care for a newborn and my post natal self. After all, I had survived the rigors of infertility treatments. What could be worse? I had thought my problem was getting pregnant, but once I got past that, the rest would be smooth sailing. Post natal depression altered my perspective. It was as if I'd been in an awful, freak car accident, one where I flew headfirst into the windshield through which I had viewed my life for the past thirty-seven years. Suddenly, not only could I not do the thing I planned on doing (raising a child), but I couldn't handle any aspect of it. The frightening part was that I didn't even want to try. Somehow I felt responsible for the predicament I was in, but I also felt it was futile to attempt to improve my situation. I was too unhappy to believe it could ever get better.

The unfortunate part is that I was never seriously educated about the fact that post natal depression might occur. It is very real and has quietly devastated the lives of many people. If I had been better informed, I might not have considered myself a candidate, but at least I would have been armed with some important information. I am incredibly thankful to have recognized early on that something was wrong and that I was able to find help. I hate to think about the women who endure this type of depression for long periods of time without knowing that there is assistance available.

Nonetheless, looking back, I wish I'd handled things differently. For starters, I wish I'd been more open to hearing what my friends were saying when they first started talking to me about post natal depression. That way perhaps I would have better appreciated that I was at risk. And although my therapist was extremely helpful, I wish I hadn't waited until I was in California to seek professional help. There are psychiatrists who specialize in treating this illness, and I should have sought one out right away. I wish I hadn't gone off the medicine so cavalierly when we were back in California. Clearly that was *not* the right thing to do! Finally, I wish I hadn't gone to make that movie in Sacramento. Although it was professionally rewarding, it was extremely taxing, and I now realize that it might have been too soon to be taking on such a project. In addition, disrupting the therapeutic process was not a good idea.

I HAVE COME so far in my love for and appreciation of my unique and incredible child. Instead of feeling numb to her or envisioning her being hurt in some way, I now crave her and want to protect her with my life. I revel in all of her behaviors (well, the cute ones, anyway), and each one of her "tricks" makes me proud. Whether she is giving flyaway kisses, or hailing a taxi with her chubby little arm in the air, I am filled with happiness. When she spontaneously gives me one of her openmouthed kisses or rests her cheek on my bare stomach, I am able to be in the moment and enjoy it.

Sometimes I feel like I literally can't get enough of her and would inhale her into my lungs and pour her through my veins if I could. The closest I came to actually succeeding at this was when I accidentally gave her a hickey. One morning after her nap, I was smothering her with kisses. Later I noticed on her neck a reddish mark with tiny black and blue spots. I panicked, thinking she had been bitten or had fallen somehow. After retracing our steps, I realized I was the culprit. I laughed at my carelessness and the fact that I wanted to devour my tasty girl. As I had sat wailing in my bed those long months ago, I never would have believed I could feel this way. You know, the odd thing is that I have never even given Chris a hickey like that!

The animal instincts that pop up during motherhood have begun to fascinate me. For instance, the other day, just like a mother bird, I began chewing bits of Rowan's food in my own mouth before giving them to her to eat. Another time, Rowan had fallen and cut her mouth. As I was comforting her, I kissed her bloody little lip, and the metallic taste of the blood made me weak in the knees. She was already feeling better, but I had to sit down with her still in my arms to stop the dizziness. It surprised me that I had such a physical response to her pain. I was reminded of how, when we'd just brought her home from the hospital, the smell of the plastic on her diaper had made me feel ill. What a contrast this situation presented!

I can't believe she is my child. I ache at how intelligent and truly perfect Rowan is. She is pure and stunningly beautiful both inside and out. I acknowledge that everyone has the perfect child; I have simply added myself to the list. When Rowan reaches out for me, or when she runs across the room to snuggle into my chest, I know I exist, and my life feels complete. In this sense, motherhood seems both selfish and selfless. She gives me purpose and makes me feel more special than I have ever felt, yet at the same time, I would die for her. As I recall the dark thoughts I had when I was really depressed and wanting to take my own life, I am moved by this distinction: I considered taking my own life, and now I would give it away if it were for her benefit.

Although being a mother is not the only thing I am, it further defines me. I realize I can be a mother and have a career. I think I feared losing myself when I had a child, and the post natal only made it worse. Now I see that I've gained even more of who I am. Life never gets boring, and although I am tired pretty much all the time, Rowan never stops inspiring me. Whether she's making me want to become a better mom, a stronger wife, or a more honest actress, I hold her in my thoughts.

I may have doubted it before, but I now know that I do deserve to be a mother. Even though I am far from perfect, I am doing my best. I dread the inevitable day when Rowan blames me for everything wrong in her life, but I'll jump off that bridge when I come to it. For now she thinks I can make it rain, and I am letting her believe that for as long as I can.

The most remarkable part about this entire experience is that I want to have another child. I look at the early photos of the two of us, and I can remember the pain; the gravity of my situation is often visible in my expression. I can see my fear and the vacant look about which my mother-in-law spoke. I was depressed and needed medical help. Now I understand that my severe unhappiness stemmed from a medical condition. Coping with the monumental, life-altering change that occurs when you have a baby is traumatic, even under the best of circumstances, but add in post natal and I became desperate.

But as I look at these photos, I also see the beauty in my baby girl and in our relationship. There are signs of my progress. My eyes gradually became more alive, and things really did get better. Life eventually evened out for all of us, and although there will always be ups and downs, I am assured that I can get through them. In preparation for this next step, I've been gradually weaning myself off the medication I've been taking, but this time I'm doing it under the guidance of my physician. Now, not only do I feel more prepared, but I feel strengthened by the experience.

IT IS SEVEN A.M. on May 15, 2004, another bright Manhattan morning. It is also Rowan's first birthday, and she has just woken up. She has a very sleepy face, and her hair is going in every direction. She reaches out for me to pick her up, which I do, sneaking a huge kiss in the process. Rowan doesn't know that it is her birthday; nor does she even understand what a birthday is. Chris and I have stayed up until the wee hours decorating our apartment to look like we are underwater. The theme of her party is Finding Nemo, *and the place is filled with orange balloons and blue and orange fish lights. I rock my sleepy baby in the rocking chair for a while and explain to her that Mommy and Daddy have a fun day planned for the birthday girl. I describe the party in detail and although she doesn't have a clue what I am saying, she smiles up at me anyway. Once she is fed and dressed, she sees the decorations. As she toddles through what looks like a sea of balloons, she squeals with joy. I realize I am more excited about this party than I have ever been for one of my own. It also crosses my mind that a child's first birthday party is actually more for the parents than it is for the kid. We've survived the first year and get to celebrate by eating cheddar-flavored Goldfish and string cheese. Chris puts on a Nemo party hat and then puts one on me. He then says, "Watch Mommy and Daddy kiss, Rowan!" We kiss and make a loud kissing sound while our baby looks on intently. After a three-person hug, which we refer to as "The Bronx Squeeze," it is time to get down to serious party business. We put the food out on the table with crumpled tissue paper doubling as sand. Soon the guests start to arrive.*

The party is in full force, and the birthday girl is dressed in a white sleeveless tulle party dress and a plastic silver tiara that says HAPPY BIRTHDAY *on it. Miraculously, she has kept the tiara on her head and is running around grabbing at balloons and jabbering continuously in her own special language. Suddenly someone accidentally steps on the Barney doll that I had quickly passed from Rowan on to our dog, Darla, and "Itsy Bitsy Spider" starts to play from its purple body. Just as suddenly Rowan plops down, stretches out her bare little arms in front of her, and begins to mime the actions in the song. I know Rowan knows some of the movements because we do the song often and she mimics parts of it, but I have never seen her do all of them by herself, without our prompting. Rowan remembers every hand motion to every portion of the song. I stare in amazement as her chubby baby hands with their dimpled knuckles intertwine while she pretends to be the spider climbing up the water spout. I can't help myself and, plopping myself down in front of her, I quickly join in the song. While the guests and their parents are all playing with pails and shovels and eating Nemo cookies, my daughter and I finish the verse. With tears filling my eyes, we both reach up our hands and float them down like raindrops in front of us. As our fingers touch, I whisper, "Down came the rain and washed the spider out. Out came the sun and dried up all the rain, and the itsy bitsy spider went up the spout again."*

AFTERWORD

If you think you might be suffering from any kind of post natal mood disorder, or are aware of some preexisting condition in your life that could lead to it, DO NOT WASTE TIME! Get help right away. Even if you don't have a history of depression or haven't experienced any of the aforementioned precipitating events, but what you are feeling seems to reach beyond those few days of symptoms associated with the baby blues, then consult a professional. Don't be ashamed and don't disregard what you are feeling. It is better to be proactive. Post natal depression is extremely treatable, and there are many ways to cope with and get through it. It is important to get educated and to talk about how you are feeling. It rarely passes alone or without causing damage.

And remember: post natal depression is beyond your control. It is very real and is more common than most people realize. You need not be a hero. Having it does not mean you are not a good mother or that you are crazy. Above all, it does not mean you don't love your child. There is no reason to feel embarrassed or guilty or to believe that it is something you should be able to soldier through on your own. Help is available in various forms. If you're not comfortable talking about it with your friends or family, then speak to your doctor privately. The most important thing is that you don't wait for it to pass. Most likely it will only get worse and cause more damage. I recovered only because I got help. Why waste time feeling horrible when you can take advantage of the assistance available?

Here are some resources to get you started:

Books

- *Beyond the Blues: A Guide to Understanding and Treating Prenatal and Postpartum Depression*, by Shoshana S. Bennett, Ph.D., and Pec Indman, Ed.D., MFT. San Jose, CA: Moodswings Press, 2003.
- *This Isn't What I Expected: Overcoming Postpartum Depression*, by Karen Kleiman, M.S.W., and Valerie D. Raskin, M.D. New York: Bantam Books, 1994.
- *The Darkest Days of My Life: Stories of Postpartum Depression*, by Natasha S. Mauthner. Cambridge, MA: Harvard University Press, 2002.
- *Mothering the New Mother: Women's Feelings and Needs After Childbirth, a Support and Resource Guide*, by Sally Placksin. New York: Newmarket Press, 2000.
- *When Words Are Not Enough: The Women's Prescription for Depression and Anxiety*, by Valerie Davis Raskin, M.D. New York: Broadway Books, 1997.

- *How to Make a New Mother Happy: A Doctor's Guide to Solving Her Most Common Problems—Quickly and Effectively*, by Uzzi Reiss, M.D., and Yfat M. Reiss. San Francisco, CA: Chronicle Books, 2004.

- *Conquering Postpartum Depression: A Proven Plan for Recovery*, by Ronald Rosenberg, M.D., Deborah Greening, Ph.D., and James Windell, M.A. Cambridge, MA: Da Capo Press, 2004.

- *Overcoming Postpartum Depression and Anxiety*, by Linda Sebastian. Omaha, NE: Addicus Books, 1998.

- *Women's Moods: What Every Woman Must Know About Hormones, the Brain, and Emotional Health*, by Deborah Sichel, M.D., and Jeanne Watson Driscoll, M.D., R.N., C.S. New York: Quill, 2000.

Websites

- www.aafp.org, the American Academy of Family Physicians; see also www.familydoctor.org/x2296.xml, "Postpartum Depression and the 'Baby Blues.'"

- www.acog.com, the American College of Obstetricians and Gynecologists

- www.apa.org, the American Psychological Association

- www.depressionafterdelivery.com, Depression After Delivery, Inc.

- www.4woman.gov/faq/postpartum.htm, the National Women's Health Information Center, a Project of the U.S. Department of Health and Human Services, Office on Women's Health

- www.healthieryou.com/postpart.html, Continuing Medical Education

- www.KidsHealth.org, the Nemours Foundation

- www.nimh.nih.gov, National Institute of Mental Health

- www.nmha.org, the National Mental Health Association

- www.postpartumassistance.com, Post natal Assistance for Mothers

- www.postpartum.net, Post natal Support International

- www.wellmother.com, WellMother.Com
- www.womensmentalhealth.org, the Massachusetts General Hospital Center for Women's Mental Health

---

HOTLINES

- **911**
- **1-800-PPD-MOMS (1-800-773-6667)**
- **1-800-SUICIDE (1-800-784-2433)**
